The Art of Success
10 Steps to Transform Your Life

Malcolm McCrae

Table of Contents

4   Dedication

5   Acknowledgments

7   How To Use This Book

8   Introduction

22   Passion - Find your purpose

34   Vision - See beyond your current situation

46   Successful Mindset - Believe, Overcome, Compete, Study, Focus

58   Value - Establish your worth. Time is money

70   Mentorship - Find and be a coach, mentor or guru

82   Courage - Overcoming adversity. Don't take "no" for an answer

96   Goals - Plan your success. Failure is not an option

108   Consistency - Success is a blueprint. Failure is a habit

120   Entrepreneurship - Your business supports your lifestyle

132   Leadership - How to discover the true leader inside of you

144   Appendix

Dedication

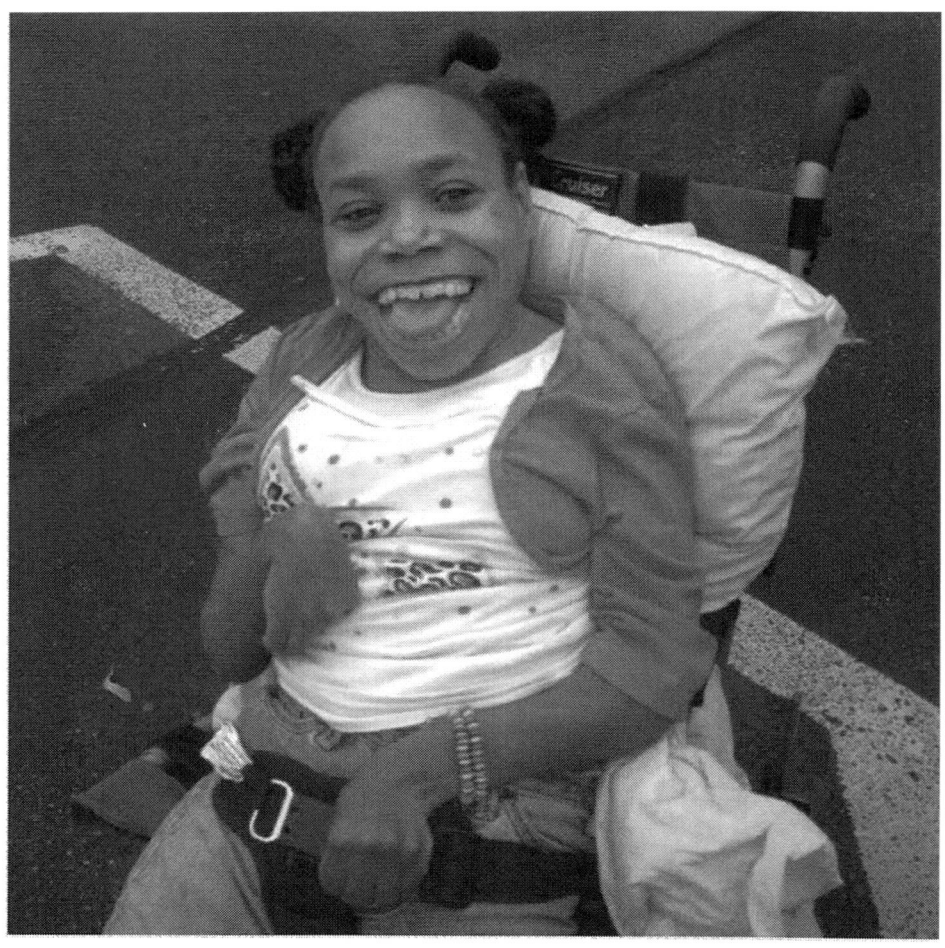

To my dearly departed sister, Omotiyo Agbongbon, thank you for teaching me how to smile and watching over us all through this journey

Acknowledgments

I would like to give special thanks to my dear wife, Natalie McCrae, for believing in me through this process.

Thank you to my father, Pops, for proof reading every chapter and giving me your wisdom and input.

Special thanks to my editor, Brian Noto, and his wife, Dr. Quantella Noto, without their support I couldn't have done this.

Redonna Rodgers, Betty Jackson-McCrae, my brothers and sisters, Fayomi, Adubifa, Omotiyo, and Nandi, my daughter Zakiya McCrae, Edward Gordon, DeVon Dent, Antonio Felder, Chike Akua, Beverly Fletcher, Danny Roach, Josh Ray, Moses McCrae and the McCrae family.

Thanks to Valentina A. Tetteh, NCC, St. Lawrence University.

To the ancestors who paved the way for my success; Baba Ogun and the Orisha, Andre Moore, C.J. Madame Walker, Louis Armstrong, Muhammad Ali, Billie Holiday, John Johnson.

How To Use This Book

I wrote this book as a guide to your success. As a successful artist, author, entrepreneur and speaker I felt I had a responsibility to help others fulfill their dreams and to find the greatness in their lives.

I have enjoyed the experience of mentoring dozens of dreamers, business people and creatives in my artistic life. I also travel the world sharing my message of living, creating and inspiring with teachers and students as well as entrepreneurs and corporations at live events.

As part of this mentoring process I've had the opportunity to share the tools of my success with many people. Once it occurred to me that this knowledge had been so transforming for them, I wanted to share it with others around the world.

Use this book as a "survival guide' on your personal path to success. While on this journey take the proper steps to honestly record your progress as well as your failures and obstacles. This documentation process is vital and must be recorded in great detail with times, dates, locations, feelings and outcomes.

In this book I share the personal stories that have helped me become a better father and husband and have helped me achieve my dreams and goals in business. I also incorporate the mentors and role models that have shared their lives and experience while guiding me on my journey.

To best digest this information I recommend reading this book two times. First, straight through taking the time to reflect on how you can adapt these tools to your life. When reading the second time have pen and paper available to write notes and ideas that may inspire you. Each chapter was written to help you create your road map to success.

Use this tool to ignite your passion, create your success and transform your life.

Introduction

My name is Malcolm McCrae. I am an artist, author, educator and entrepreneur. I travel the world inspiring people to be the greatest version of themselves. I was born in 1980 in Milwaukee, Wisconsin, the oldest of five children. I got my discipline, focus and courageous spirit from my mom and dad. My mom was an incredible woman. She was very loving, protective and nurturing when it came to her family as well as helping others. She would go above and beyond to support folks in their time of need. Growing up while watching her raise five kids made me realize that anything is possible when you put your mind to it.

When people think of Milwaukee they think of beer, cheese and brats. But this couldn't be farther from the truth. Milwaukee is the most segregated city in the United States.[1] One of the things I remember from an early age was a lack of black men in my community: fathers, uncles, brothers, nephews. I was too young to know it, but in many cases, once they were in handcuffs they were never coming back. Wisconsin has the highest percentage of incarcerated black men among all 50 states.[1] By age 34, 62-percent of men in one Milwaukee urban zip code have spent time in an adult state correctional facility.[1]

The odds were stacked against me, except for one thing. I was lucky enough to have my father around. My father was an art teacher at the Boys and Girls Club in Milwaukee. Not only was my dad an art teacher, he was an art teacher in one of the roughest areas in Milwaukee; Hillside Public Housing. The projects, the hood, the ghetto. They called him Mr. BaBa which means father in many African cultures. More than an art teacher, he was more like a caring father to his students and often their families. Many times as a young man I would find myself in social settings where a stranger would show me their respect and appreciation for my father through some act of kindness. The conversations always began with, "Are you Mr. BaBa's son"?

My dad was the first person that really showed me not only is caring important, but how creativity can be used as a tool. He used this as a tool to heal and deal with some of the wounds with which these young people were dealing. I was that young person, too.

---

[1] Pawasarat, John and Quinn, Lois M., "Wisconsin's Mass Incarceration of African-American Males, Summary" (2014) *ETI Publications*. Paper 10. http://dc.uwm.edu/eti_pubs/10

"A network of bridges separates Milwaukee. Hispanics and Latinos live on the south side. The east side is the upscale, white area where the University of Wisconsin Milwaukee is located. The west side is a more suburban area outside of the city. The north side of town is the black, inner city area."

Passage from "To Live, To Create, To Inspire", - Malcolm McCrae

By age 34, 62-percent of men in one Milwaukee urban zip code have spent time in an adult state correctional facility. Malcolm snapped this photo on a 2016 visit capturing the aftermath of a homicide.

Looking back now on my life, as a man, and somebody who really cares about inspiring the next generation of leaders, I realize why it was so important for him to be an art teacher in an area like Hillside.

The Hillside Boys and Girls Club was a magical place where I could just draw out all the pain and frustration with which I was dealing. My parents were going through a divorce and it was really painful for me. I was trying to figure out if it was my fault. Or was it their fault? For some reason I felt like this responsibility and pain was my fault. I can remember dealing with this situation deep inside myself. The only way that I could deal with it all was to draw it out.

My journey as a creative began at a young age. But not without problems. I was the 10-year old kid in school that was being disrespectful and disruptive in class. At a young age I was labeled with Attention Deficit Hyperactivity Disorder (ADHD). I was the kid that was at the back of the class throwing paper and getting in trouble a lot.

One day an art teacher came to me. She saw something in me that was bigger than being a disruptive kid and gave me an opportunity to deal with some of my emotions and pain. She gave me a pencil and paper and just let me draw it out. I realized that I wanted to make things. Making things helped me not cover up the pain but work through it.

It was only through art that I found an outlet. I wouldn't be here today if it wasn't for those times in my life. The passion and commitment was beginning to develop through my upbringing and adult role models.

I had been drawing but I wanted more. I wanted to do something else. I wanted to take my art form to the next level. I didn't know how to do that. I remember walking through the mall and seeing this guy airbrushing T-shirts. It was the first time I saw street art being put on different surfaces. I instantly knew this is what I wanted to do, to become an airbrush artist.

So I took all of my drawings and went home and compounded them into a portfolio. As a kid I didn't know what a portfolio was so I just took all of my work. I remember feeling so prideful, going up there showing this guy my work. He starts to go through the papers and he's taking his time. I was

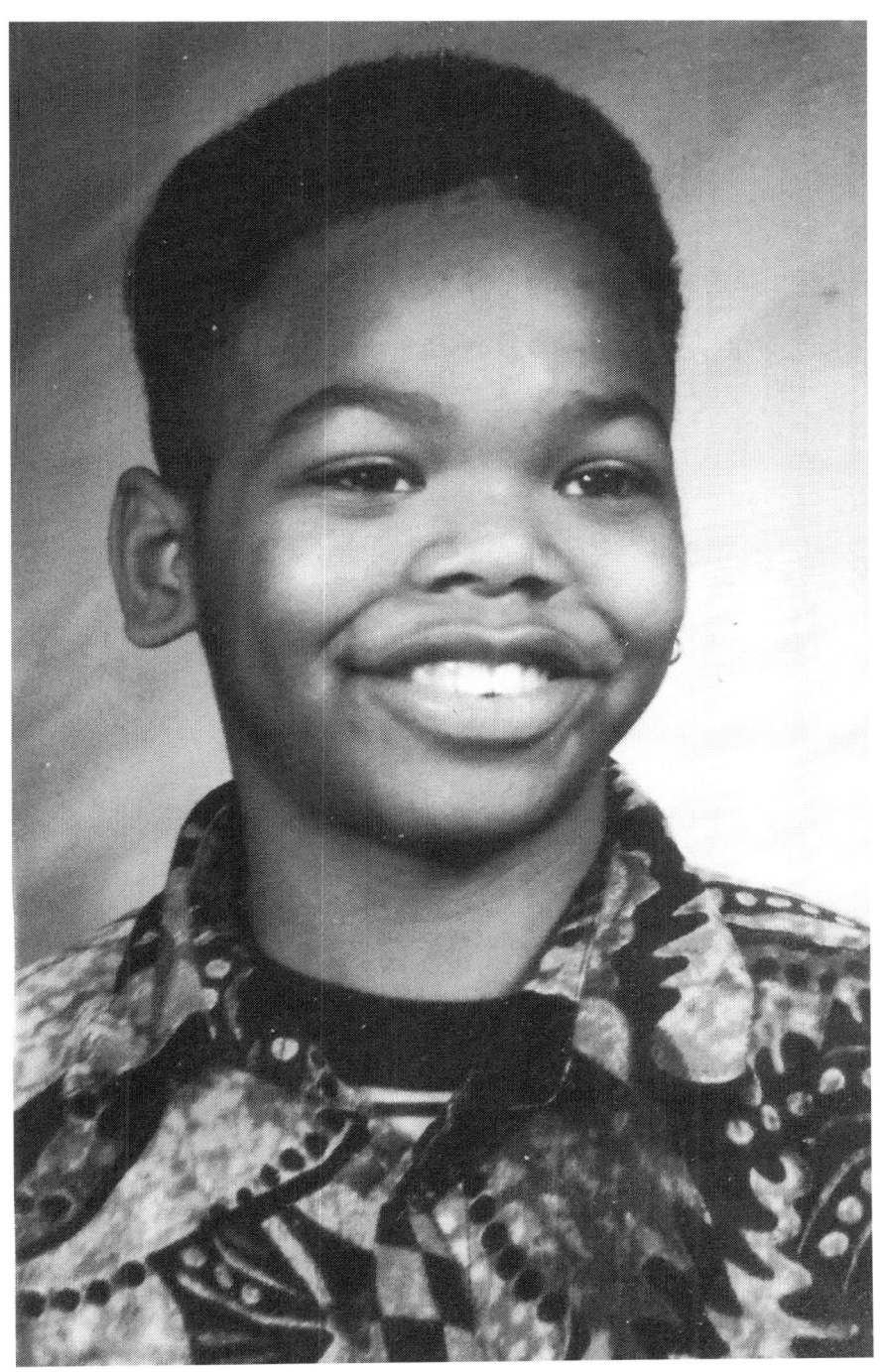

thinking "Yes, I aced it." And then he totally just destroyed and crushed my whole dream by telling me, "Your work is great, but I just really don't have time to train anybody or babysit any body's kid." I'm going to be honest. I was heartbroken. I mean this was the first time that I had to really deal with rejection in my work and somebody telling me, "no." I had to make a decision. I could move forward towards something that I really wanted to do or give myself excuses to be a victim or a casualty.

Milwaukee is one of the roughest, most segregated cities in America and the majority of the people that I grew up with, I mean about 70% of the people that I probably graduated high school with, are incarcerated or dead. At that point in time, I remember thinking that if I didn't follow what my heart and my dreams and my ambitions and my soul was telling me, that I could've easily fallen into the same trap. I was dealing with a lot during this transition.

Here we are, my mom and my dad were broken up. They were going through a divorce and fighting a lot. I'm the oldest out of five. One of my little sisters had cerebral palsy. A lot of the pressure was on me as the oldest to be able to watch my brother and sisters when my mom was at work. My mom ended up sending me to go live with my dad. She packed up all of my stuff and we went to the airport and she put me on a plane to Ohio.

My dad came to pick me up from the airport in Columbus. This is the furthest away I had been from home. We got in a cab and I remember just riding for awhile looking out the window. I start noticing we were going through the hood. We pull up to this big building on the right side. My dad tells me to put my bag in the room. My brother Dubi, who was already in Columbus, said not to put it on the floor because the rats would go through it. He takes my bag and hangs it on a hook in a closet. I remember I was so tired. I couldn't even imagine rats going through my bags.

I went to the bathroom. My first reaction was to turn on the light. I found the switch and turned it on, but there was no power. I ran out of the bathroom and frantically started to turn on all the switches in the house. Dubi starts shaking his head and said, "There's no electricity." I said, "What?" Reality hit me. My dad and brother were living in an abandoned building!

To Live, To Create, To Inspire Book

Malcolm McCrae depicts his journey from sleeping in abandoned buildings in the unforgiving Ohio winters to his rise as a successful artist, educator, speaker and author. Malcolm shares his practical values for success, and how art and creativity had saved his life as an at risk youth. These lessons can be applied to the readers life no matter the background, environment, or circumstances. The book not only details his struggles and successes but it also provides invaluable insight on how anyone can use their sense of creativity to accomplish their dreams.

www.MalcolmMccrae.com

My dad, my brother and I lived in an abandoned building for two years with no electricity, no heat, and no running water. I had to make another decision. Was I going to go call home and cry to mom that we don't have this or we don't have that, or was I going to man up? In the African culture, the time when you go from boyhood to manhood is called a rite of passage. I knew that my dad wasn't going to send me through anything I couldn't handle. I remember that night asking my father what happened. He told me "This is life son. This is what you've got to go through sometimes, the ups and downs."

What I did bring with me was my airbrush, my art materials and some clothes. Since the building was abandoned people didn't know we lived there. There was a bus stop on the corner and people would be sitting on the front stairs. One day my dad was like, "Well, why don't you just set up an easel on the stairs and while they're sitting there, they can buy your shirts." And so I set up and made my first $100 on that stoop.

15

During the time we were homeless living in that building, my father, brother and I had one vision and one dream and that was to create a successful business. We dreamed of living upstairs in the building and downstairs we would run the business. That was our number one dream.

I remember one morning someone knocking on our door. We didn't have a phone and it was one of the employees that worked at the corner store where my dad worked. He came to get my dad and he left for a couple of hours. He came back and told me and my brother that my mom was in the hospital. She had a blood clot in her lung. Of course, we're like okay well you know she's going to be alright. But the reality is my mom died that day and immediately we hopped on a plane to get to Milwaukee to take care of the girls. We get there and I had to make another decision. Was I going to continue on with my vision?

At 17 years old, we created a business called Sho' Time Wild Image. My dad, brother and I found a building that had a storefront downstairs and living quarters upstairs. It was perfect. The exact building that we needed. We opened the business on a shoe string budget The first two years were tough, but after the third year we were making over $75,000. By the fifth year we were grossing over $150,000 a year. We had over 10 employees and were creating some of the hottest wearable art in the world! I was able to even establish a license deal with a company in Australia.

I created this successful business of doing airbrush and screen printing but there was a catch. Ninety-percent of the work that I was doing was built around memorial T-shirts. Death shirts mostly for the black and Latino communities. We would get photos of the departed, print them out on T-shirts and have sayings commemorating them. So here I am, a young creative guy making a lot of money, but something wasn't right. I was spending 90% of my business, 90% of my time, dealing with death. It was depressing hearing the stories of death especially of young men. I had to remember that my goal and my whole nature was built around art and creativity which is an uplifting spirit. I had to make a decision. I knew what it meant to have money, but I didn't know what true success was.

After years of success with Sho' Time Wild Image I became very unhappy with the business structure. I became tired and burned out of the

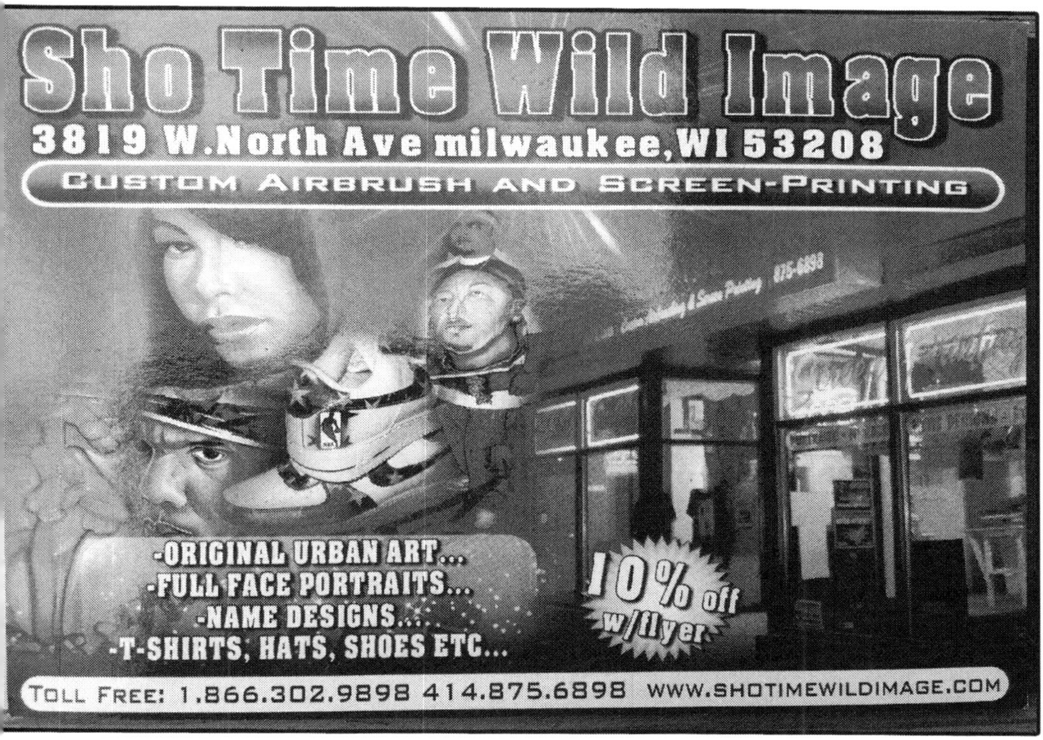
Sho Time Wild Image
3819 W.North Ave milwaukee,WI 53208
CUSTOM AIRBRUSH AND SCREEN-PRINTING
-ORIGINAL URBAN ART...
-FULL FACE PORTRAITS...
-NAME DESIGNS....
-T-SHIRTS, HATS, SHOES ETC...
10% off w/flyer
TOLL FREE: 1.866.302.9898 414.875.6898 WWW.SHOTIMEWILDIMAGE.COM

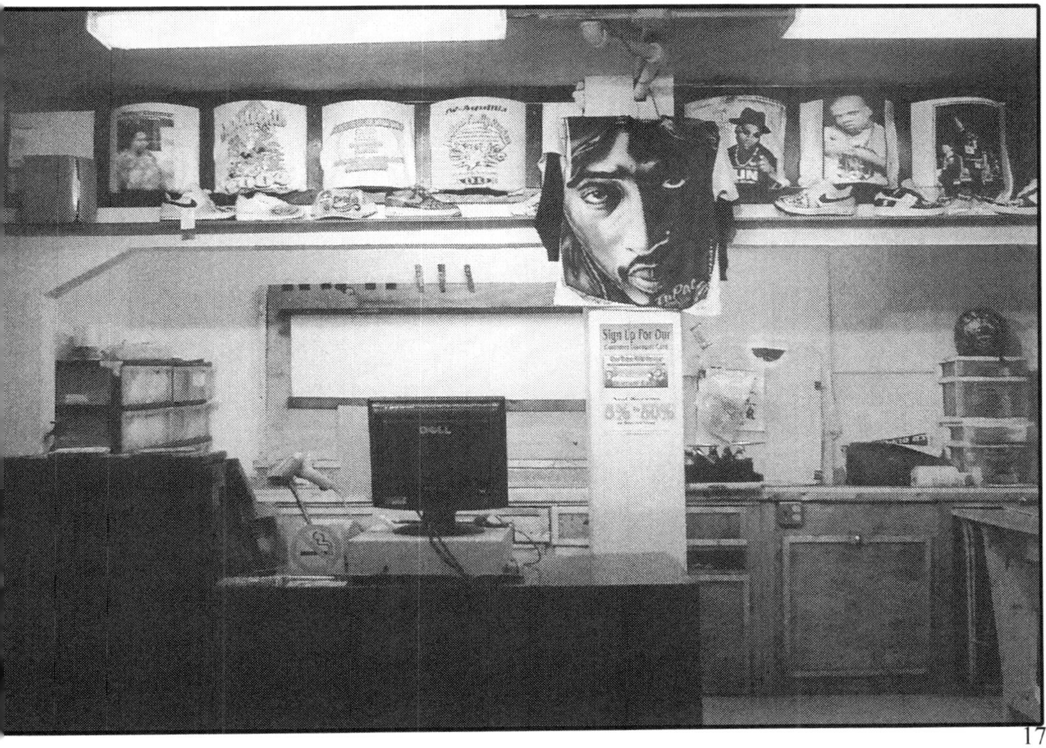
Sign Up For Our

memorial shirt market. After 10 years, I decided to close the business down in order to focus on a new direction. I was a natural born leader and wanted to share my gift of creativity with the world. I started to ask myself what did I really want to do? The answer was clear. I was motivated by helping people. I made up my mind that I needed to change the direction of my life and focus on empowering others by living, creating and inspiring.

Being a young black artist I always wanted to produce my own line of products that could be an inspiration to other young creatives of color.

I had four major goals:

My own line of airbrush DVDs.
My own airbrush gun.
My own paint that is accessible to the masses.
My own school or training facility.

I'm proud to say that I've been able to fulfill these goals. In 2014, I produced my own tool - the "Assassin Airbrush" - the first of it's kind developed by an African-American. This tool was created as an airbrush kit to be affordable for any beginner as well as professional airbrush artist. Teachers use it in schools all across the United States. As of 2017, I have produced over 12 CDs and DVDs, a series of sketchbooks, personal appearances and seminars as well as a memoir that have motivated, educated and inspired over a 100,000 students, teachers and artists across the world including Africa, England, Australia, Mexico and Germany. I've been published in trade magazines and have built a respectable career amongst my peers. The decisions that I made over 20 years ago to follow my dreams have stayed with me.

Those decisions changed my life. I now travel the world inspiring and motivating people from all walks of life. Showing them how to take something they love, and use it as a tool to make a difference. Teaching them how to have balance in life. That's the key to true success. I take pride in working with young people. I feel that it is important to share my knowledge with the next generation. I was blessed to have great people help me through my journey. I'm honored to pass along tools that I have learned. I use hip-hop, humanity and history, and incorporate them together to make that connection

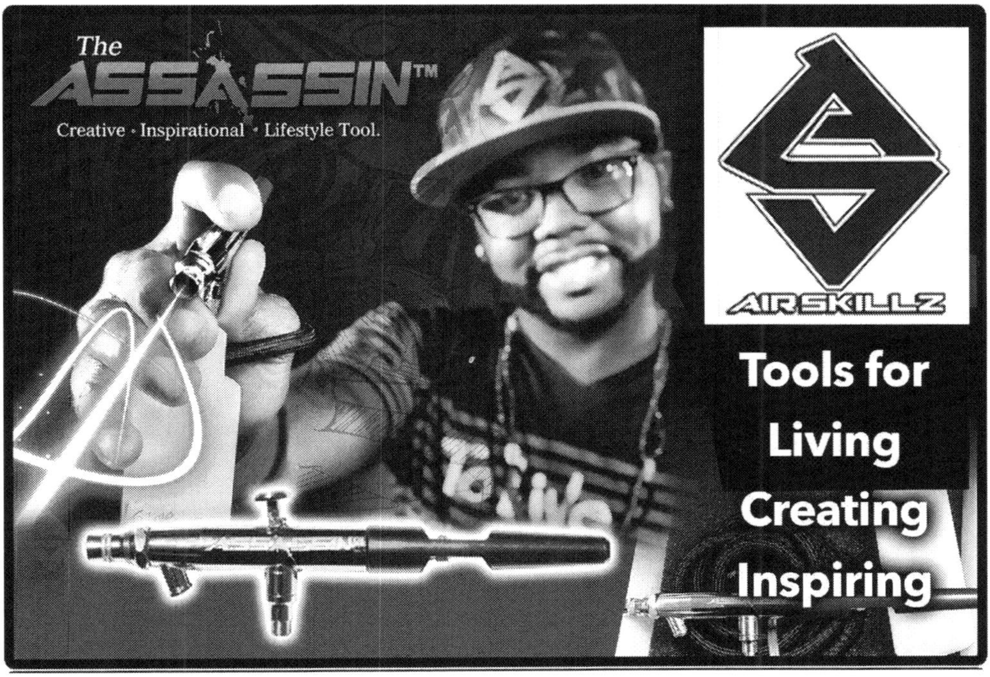
The
ASSASSIN™
Creative • Inspirational • Lifestyle Tool.
AIRSKILLZ
Tools for
Living
Creating
Inspiring

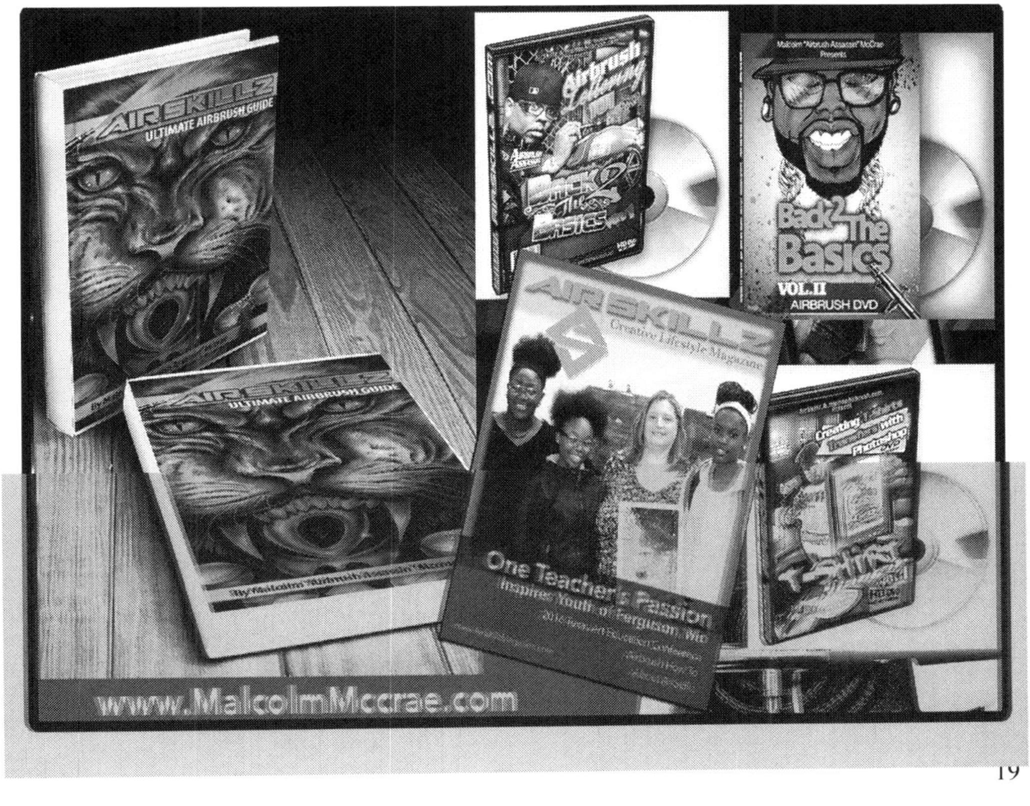
AIRSKILLZ
ULTIMATE AIRBRUSH GUIDE
Back 2 The Basics
VOL.II
AIRBRUSH DVD
AIRSKILLZ
Creative Lifestyle Magazine
One Teacher's Passion
www.MalcolmMccrae.com

with young people. Guess what? We are losing the next generation of creative professionals, not because of the schools, not because of parents, but because we aren't teaching our children to dream.

As I have been traveling the globe for the past 10 years sharing my message with thousands of educators, students and corporate clients, I have been asked certain questions that seem almost universal. The number one question I am asked is what is the secret to my success as an artist, educator, speaker and entrepreneur. One of the things I promised myself as I was going through these experiences was that someday, if I was successful, I would help others find their way. Now that I am successful I can fulfill my promise to myself.

I created this book as a tool. This is a resource that can be used in your life, business, and career. In my previous book, "*How Art Saved My Life*", I touched on my journeys where I learned these lessons. Some of which were the hard way. When I first had the idea for writing this book I wanted to focus on strategies that I learned while building a successful brand while making over $150,000 a year.

Malcolm McCrae's
Art Life Sketchbook Series

21

Chapter 1

THE ART OF
SUCCESS #AOSBOOK

www.MalcolmMccrae.com

Passion

[pash-uhn]

A strong or extravagant fondness, enthusiasm, or desire for anything.

Hye Wonnye

Find Your Passion

What is passion? Passion is that thing that pushes us to be great. I look at passion as the fuel for creativity; it helps us to determine if we're on the right track in life. When we're passionate about something we tend to do our best. At times, passion pushes us to move forward to make the necessary steps towards success. We see passion everyday when we watch sports. The most successful athletes are the most passionate. We love the way Michael Jordan played his heart out every game in the 80's. Boxing wouldn't be the same if it weren't for the passion that Mike Tyson displayed in the ring. Passion perks the inner spirit to get up early and go to bed late. When we find our passion we find the reason we were put on this earth.

Malcolm in 1997 with soon to be Billboard Hot 100 #1 Single Artist rapper Twista at Flipside Music in Milwaukee, Wisconsin.

One of the first times that I realized I was passionate about business was when I was around 17 years old. I started to use my creativity to make money and the way that I did this was traveling to and vending at festivals. Every year I would pack a vehicle and make a 10 hour journey to Louisville, Kentucky to airbrush at the Kentucky Derby. I loved the thrill of being in the marketplace and selling my wares.

Malcolm's airbrush trailer, made out of an old Apache pop up camper, at the Kentucky Derby around 2000.

Every year I would come back determined to do better than the previous year, not only better financially but to improve my business for next time which in turn meant higher sales and profits. I was passionate to succeed and every season I would take the risk driving in a barely running vehicle to make it happen. Most times I couldn't afford a booth and I had no idea where I was going to set up. But every year I would go prepared because I knew if I would just show up, work hard, and be ready my passion would take me further than I could imagine.

What I realized was once I stepped out in public and used my passion and charisma, that would carry me through. The fear of failure became unimportant and the feeling of what the possibilities could be became all that mattered. What you have to do is allow your inner self to lead the way and the only way you can do this is to test it.

How do you know when you've found your passion? When you can do it and it doesn't feel like work. This exercise will help you to focus on your passion. Throughout this book we will use tools like this to help you construct your road map to success.

Take 10 minutes out of your day to sit down and write out things that you are passionate about, numbering them most to least important with one being the most important. It is very critical to be as specific as possible. Make a commitment to use this as a tool to push your progress ahead.

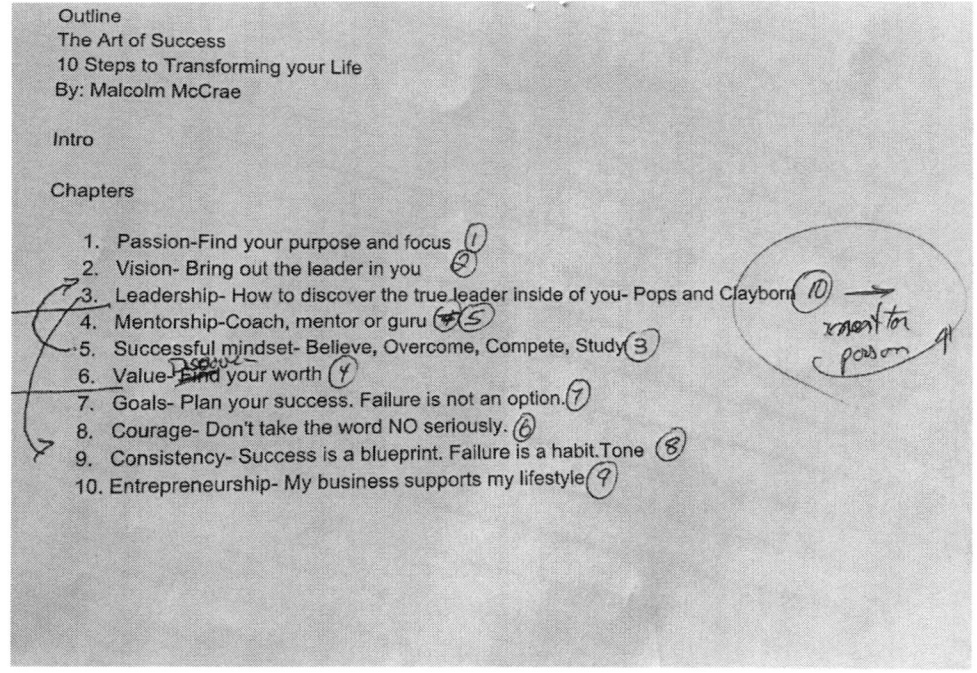

Working example of writing down chapter order and priority changes during the editing of "*The Art of Success*" book pushing the progress ahead.

"I Used To ----------!"

As I travel all over the world coaching creative people, the number one thing that I hear is "I used to do ..." It's always the same sentence; I used to draw. I used to paint. I used to sing. Most times right after the statement "I used to" people talk about what happened in their lives that stopped them from following their dream or passion. What I realized is that the person who is telling me this really wants to pursue that dream. Most times the excuse or the reason why they stopped their quest should have been the number one reason they should have stayed on their quest. Children have been the biggest excuse that most people use as a reason they stopped pursuing their dreams. Children and family should be the biggest reason that a person should push to succeed towards one's passion.

The #1 reason that I have been so successful in my journey fulfilling my career is that as a kid I saw my father work hard to follow his passions and dreams in life. So it's important for our young people to see that with a little hard work and persistence dreams can come true. We all have to have a reason why. The why gives a reason or purpose for what you're doing. Without a why you will never be successful. The why is the fire that is used to keep the heat under us; this is used to stay motivated. The number one thing that most people have to practice is consistency and not getting too comfortable. When you have a why, this helps you to stay focused, aggressive, and proactive. The sense of how you do it becomes irrelevant and a process of planning and strategy become more important. Most times we look at the end result and look how difficult a goal will be so we start over thinking things and talk ourselves out of pushing forward.

"It makes me mad when some of my friends just talk, talk, talk about what they want to do. You just need to do it, whatever it is."
- Malcolm McCrae

**Here is a quick passage from my personal journal
when I had to dig deep and
find my passion in order to continue...**

March, 9 2005

Dear journal I'm full of ideas and visions of being the best at what I do. My biggest fear is not finishing what I start. I never want to feel like it's so much work that I start to make excuses or reasons to quit. I will not allow myself a way out. At times it's hard staying motivated, but I use my passion for success to push me forward. I just finished reading the book "Multiple Streams of Internet Income" and the author is talking about this website called ebay. I think I will sell my new DVD there once it's complete. I sent out over 100 press releases to production companies and art distribution companies letting them know about my new DVD. It's been over 3 months and I haven't heard anything, yet. I'm not sure what to do. I'm on the road vending at another liquidation sale in Virginia and the money has been horrible. I've been here for two days and only sold 10 t-shirts and that will barely pay for my gas to get back home to Milwaukee. I can't wait to one day not to have to chase money....

I've been on the road for weeks and just left Tallahassee, Florida. Every weekend I feel like I'm a slave to my talent. If I don't paint hearts and names I can't eat. I'm an artist and I want to be free to create and not be in this rat race of life. I'm not complaining but I'm just a bit frustrated. I spend most of my time thinking about what I really want to do. I want to create a company and a lifestyle that will give me the financial freedom to do what I want. All I want is to share my gift. I hope that is what this DVD will do. Noone has a video teaching the urban style of airbrushing. I remember the oath I made to myself that when it was my time to share the craft of airbrushing that I wasn't going to make the same mistakes as the artists that came before me. I'm determined to make my own standards and share and grow my talent with the world. I'm on a mission to get this idea off the ground. I've been working so hard to get this DVD produced....

Earlier this week we filmed the last shot of my first urban airbrush DVD. I'm calling the new company AirSkillz. DeVon is designing the cover now. The filming we did this week was great. We had to rent over $150.00 worth of camera lights and filming equipment. It has been an expensive journey. I've spent over $1500.00 on producing this project. I was totally unprepared. My original budget was only $700.00! The videographer wants an extra $400.00 to edit the footage and I still have to pay someone to duplicate the DVD's. I'm not even sure it will sell once the DVD is complete. We finally got the last shot and I'm glad that part is over. It hasn't been easy, it's been hell. One of the hardest things that I've ever had to create has been this airbrush instructional DVD. I feel tired of hoping things will get better financially. It's hard following my dreams but I know I can't run from it because I would find myself regretting it.

Lately I've been feeling good. I feel like I got my swagga back. I just need to go with the feeling and get back on the road, but before I do I must complete a couple of things. I'm starting to realize that for me to be successful at anything that I want I must develop a system. One of my biggest problems is financial management. I'm not utilizing my money correctly. First of all, I don't pay myself first. I promised myself a budget to pay myself $400.00 per month, about $100.00 per week . I finally found a method, just like when I'm on the road and have to pay a bill. I go to the post office and get a money order and then mail it. I can use the same method. Whatever city I'm in I will take the $100 cash to the Post Office and get a money order and mail it to myself. I mail them to a P.O. Box in Milwaukee that I have. I'm now on my way to saving a bit more money in order to invest in a computer so I can film, edit and produce my own products. I'm not going to allow anyone to stop my progress. I'll let you know the progress on the next entry. Peace.

- Malcolm McCrae

Most times you will not understand or see your passion as a gift. Finding your passion is a task because most of us have been conditioned to think we can't pursue our passion because it is a dream or a fairytale. I had my issues with society trying to limit my inner voice. Most people don't have the heart or the fight to push for their happiness. When you're following your passion you have to make sure that you are listening deeply with inside your consciousness. At times you will have to find tools like audio books and self-help recordings to reprogram your subconscious thoughts. The purpose of these tools are to reinforce your positive thoughts and goals consistently in your life.

Finding your passion is one of the hardest things most of us have to do because it requires inner peace and inner reflection to find your passion. It helps us remember who and what we are. As a young person I realized I was different. I didn't have the opportunity to grow up in a wealthy household but I was raised to be self sufficient. I was raised among thinkers, entrepreneurs, artists, and visionaries. It was a great foundation for a person like me to grow up in because it always gave me an opportunity to be creative, curious and ask why.

The question "Why?" is important because it helps you to understand that there is a system to everything. As a young boy I would spend hours watching construction crews work on the streets in front of my house. I remember watching contractors build a wheelchair ramp for my little sister. From the foundation to every wood plank I was mesmerized as this structure was being created in front of me. I would always find myself staring and watching anything that was being produced by a person's hands. As an adult I realize that not only was I inspired by the creativity of building but the process one has to go to through to create a usable structure. I would watch as the contractors would study their blueprints. I would watch the tools that they used to get certain projects done and how they communicated with each other to make sure that everyone on the team was on the same page. There was always a quality control person to make sure that everything was being built to code.

I started to see that to be successful or to complete any task there are certain systems to follow. I believe that you cannot teach a person to have passion, it's within all of us. It is our responsibility to pull out the passion inside ourselves. It can be as simple as the thing that makes you feel special, unique and happy. It is a thing that should be effortless, so be patient on the journey. When you find your passion the next step is to focus in on your goals and objectives. Passion is useless without the proper focus.

Prize Winning Entrepreneur Designs his Career

By Penny McCanles

Malcolm McCrae is gearing up for his busy season. Summer means traveling to outdoor festivals with his airbrushing business. Recently he bought a van to transport his supplies, and he plans to buy a concession trailer to serve as his store when he's on the road.

Still, there are the all the things he needs to do before the summer season kicks in. Moving his business to a new location. Making sure he has enough employees to cover the counter while he's gone. Finding someone to complete the layout of his design catalog for custom skateboards, snowboards, helmets, cars and motorcycles. Getting his web page up and running. Sending his catalogs to hot rod magazines. Lately, he's been so busy doing custom auto painting that it's hard to find time for everything.

If all this isn't enough, he'll need to leave room for final exams and high school graduation. McCrae is a senior at the Milwaukee High School for Entrepreneurship.

At 18, McCrae is a gifted artist, a savvy businessman and the sole proprietor of Wild Image, located in Flip Side Records, 3716 W. North Ave. In March he received the award for Top Marketing Plan at the Young Entrepreneurs Conference and Business Competition at the Midwest Express Center, earning

a $100 cash award and a $1,000 Marquette University Scholarship.

He attributes his award to having followed his passion. "It makes me mad when some of my friends just talk, talk, talk about what they want to do. You just need to do it, whatever it is." McCrae's success may also come from the way he looks at mistakes. To his knowledge, he's never made any. "They're just things I learned from," he says.

Four years ago he began selling custom designed T-shirts at a curbside stand in Columbus, Ohio, "because my dad told me to get out there and do it." McCrae always enjoyed drawing and began
(Continued on page 6)

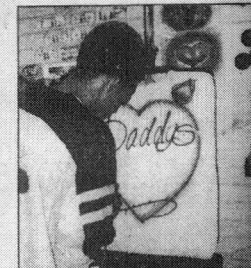

Malcolm McCrae works on a t-shirt that will eventually say "Daddy's Little Girl"

Entrepreneur, *cont. from p. 1*

airbrushing at the age of 11 after watching his uncle become frustrated and gave up. McCrae saved his money and bought his own equipment. "While other kids were playing basketball or baseball, I was at home practicing my airbrushing," he recalls. "I read about it at the library, even called people at magazines to learn about it."

Taking the Next Step
Beginning to sell his art at the curbside stand was the hardest thing he'd ever done. "I had to put my talent on the line, and I was worried people would think I wasn't good enough," he remembers. By the second day he had lost his fear and the T-shirts were selling very well. Each weekend for the rest of the

summer, he set up his stand. By fall he had earned enough to rent a booth at a flea market about eight miles from home. Each weekend during the fall and winter, McCrae and his younger brother Adubifa, then 13, would take the bus, lugging all their supplies, to sell T-shirts at the flea market.

The sudden death of his mother in Milwaukee three years ago (his parents were divorced) brought his father and the two boys back to Milwaukee to care for his younger sisters: Fayomi, then 13, Omitoyo, then 12, and Nandi, then 8.

Taking Advantage of Education
McCrae enrolled in the Milwaukee High School for the Arts. "I already knew a lot about my art, but I had never been schooled in it. School taught me about technique and the use of color." Just before his senior year, however, he transferred to the Milwaukee High School for Entrepreneurship in order to hone his business skills.

On the basis of his portfolio, he found space for his business in Upper Echelon, a shop on Martin Luther King Drive, and another at Flip Side Music. He added a third space at Pack It In Productions across from the Grand Avenue Mall, but later abandoned two of the spaces when managing so many employees became too stressful.

Now McCrae limits his retail space to the North Avenue location, selling custom T-shirts, sweatshirts, bibs, key chain tags, visors and license plates. Recently he's begun to spend a good

deal of his time away from the store doing custom auto painting. His three or four employees take care of the shop when he's away; but he realizes that as he's absent more and more, he needs an employee who will invest himself in the business, "who will be here for the long term."

> *"It makes me mad when some of my friends just talk, talk, talk about what they want to do. You just need to do it, whatever it is."*
> *— Malcolm McCrae*

Family Partnerships
In late June, McCrae will move his store into his father's printing shop across the street from his present location. The family already lives upstairs of the shop, so working there will be convenient. Also, McCrae looks forward to some cooperative ventures with his father. He wants to develop a line of outlines that his father will then print on transfer paper for other airbrush artists to use. The transfers can be ironed onto T-shirts, then filled in with an airbrush.

Right now, McCrae is enjoying the flexibility that his entrepreneurial position allows. One day he's in the shop; the next he may be creating a backdrop for a photo shoot or working on a car. But eventually he'd like to be able to "take care of" his employees. "I want to pay them better and provide benefits for them," he explains. At the rate he's going, that may not be long.

Newspaper article from the June-July, 1999 edition of the Sherman Park Today! (Milwaukee, WI) describing the then 18 year-old Malcolm McCrae's passion.

"There are those who spend their lives studying it and those who spend their lives doing it."

-Ernie Hudson

Malcolm with playwright, producer and veteran film and television actor Ernie Hudson who is perhaps best known for his roles as Winston Zeddemore in the *Ghostbusters* film series, Sergeant Darryl Albrecht in *The Crow* (1994) and Warden Leo Glynn on HBO's *Oz*.

Chapter 2

THE ART
SUCCESS #AOSBOOK

www.MalcolmMccrae.com

Vision
[vizh-uhn]

A thought, concept, or object
formed by the imagination.

Sesa woruban

The Ability To See Beyond Your Current Situation

Have a vision of change and innovation. Don't go with the fad... create the fad. This is one of the traps of being a creative thinker; we start thinking too much. Sometimes over thinking can be the worst thing a creative person can do. The easy thing is to follow what we feel society wants. They want little butterflies, so we paint butterflies. You see this thinking a lot in the music industry; there is no originality. Artists follow whatever is played on the radio; if this summer it's hardcore rap then everyone is a gangster, rapping about shooting guns and selling dope. The easy way to do anything is to follow the leader. It takes risk to find and build your own style and brand.

Malcolm's vision of the urban airbrush movement helped him establish himself as a leader through innovation and brand building.

The people who create their own style create their own destiny. They will always be known as the original while others will be remembered as copies or knockoffs. In this day and age you can find thousands of trends or fads, especially on the Internet. People are looking not only for a service or product but also an experience. You have to go from creative to innovative. Thinking outside of the box makes eyes pop and dollars drop. In the business we call it the pop and wow. What is your pop and wow? What makes you different? Why should someone dig in their pockets and spend their hard earned cash with you? What makes you special? Asking these questions is what helped make Apple in to a multi-billion dollar company. The answers to these questions is what makes you go from ordinary to extraordinary.

"You spend so much time in your profession it ought to be something you love."

- John Johnson

One of my favorite entrepreneurs who had incredible vision to build a media empire was John Johnson, founder of Johnson Publishing which became the largest black-owned publishing company in the world. While reading his autobiography *"Succeeding Against the Odds"*, Johnson shares how having vision was a very important asset to his success. In 1982, he became the first African-American to appear on the Forbes 400. Johnson's Ebony and Jet magazines were among the most influential African-American businesses in media in the second half of the twentieth century.

Johnson was born in rural Arkansas City, Arkansas, the grandson of slaves. When he was six years old, his father died in a sawmill accident and Johnson was raised by his mother and stepfather. He attended an overcrowded and segregated elementary school. Such was his love of learning, that he repeated the eighth grade rather than discontinue his education as there was no public high school for African-Americans in his community. After a visit with his mother to Chicago World's Fair, they decided that opportunities

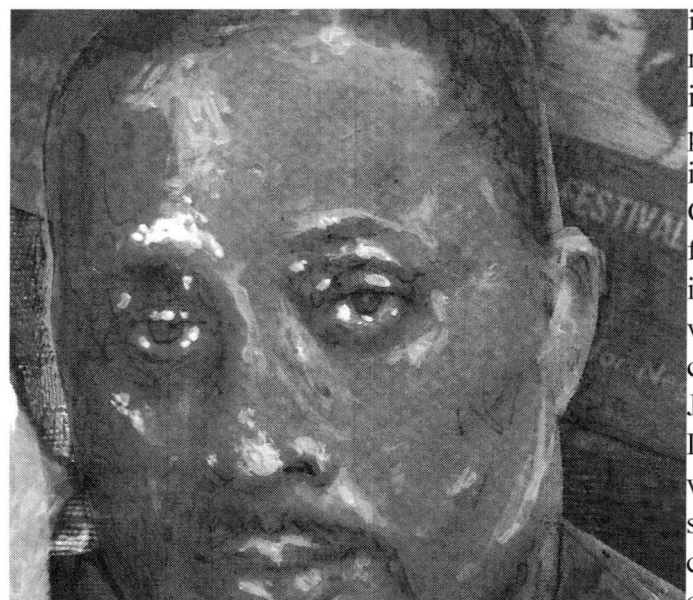 in the North were more plentiful than in the South. Facing poverty on every side in Arkansas during the Great Depression, the family moved to Chicago in 1933 to try to find work and for Johnson to continue his education. Johnson entered all black DuSable High School while his mother and stepfather scoured the city for jobs during the day. He looked for work after school and during the summer as well, but without success. His mother was not even able to find any domestic work, which was generally available when all else failed. To support themselves, the family applied for welfare, which they received for two years until Johnson's stepfather was finally able to obtain a position with the Works Progress Administration (WPA) and Johnson himself secured a job with the National Youth Administration (NYA).

John Johnson was a businessman and publisher. He was the founder of the Johnson Publishing Company. In 1982, he became the first African-American to appear on the Forbes 400. Johnson's Ebony and Jet magazines were among the most influential African-American businesses in media in the second half of the twentieth century.

Ebony was so popular that its initial run of 25,000 copies easily sold out. The articles in Ebony, which were designed to look like those in Life or Look magazines, emphasized the achievements of successful African-Americans.

Johnson endured much teasing and taunting at his high school for his ragged clothes and country ways as he encountered something he never knew existed; middle-class blacks. At DuSable High School his classmates included Nat King Cole, Redd Foxx and future entrepreneur William Abernathy. This only fueled his already formidable determination to "make something of himself." Johnson's high-school career was distinguished by the leadership qualities he demonstrated as student council president and as editor of the school newspaper and class yearbook. He attended high school during the day and studied self-improvement books at night. After he graduated in 1936, he was offered a tuition scholarship to the University of Chicago, but he thought he would have to decline it because he could not figure out a way to pay for expenses other than tuition. Because of his achievements in high school, Johnson was invited to speak at a dinner held by the Urban League. When Harry Pace, president of the Supreme Life Insurance Company, heard Johnson's speech, he was so impressed with the young man that he offered Johnson a job so that he would be able to use the scholarship.

Johnson began as an office boy at Supreme Life and within two years had become Pace's assistant. His duties included preparing a monthly digest of newspaper articles. Johnson began to wonder if other people in the community might not enjoy the same type of service. He conceived of a publication patterned after Reader's Digest. His work at Supreme Life gave him the opportunity to see the day-to-day operations of a business owned by an African-American and fostered his dream of starting a business of his own.

Ebony Magazine

Ebony, was so popular that its initial run of 25,000 copies easily sold out. The articles in Ebony, which were designed to look like those in Life or Look magazines, emphasized the achievements of successful African-Americans. Photo essays about current events and articles about race relations were also included in the magazine. Initially focused on the rich and famous in the African-American community, Johnson expanded the reporting to include issues such as "the white problem in America", African-American militancy, crimes by African-Americans against African-Americans, civil rights legislation, freedom rides and marches, and other aspects of segregation and discrimination.

Ebony Magazine made a conscious effort to portray positive aspects of African-American life and culture. Johnson maintained that Ebony's success was due to the positive image of African Americans that it offered.

Professional historians were recruited for the magazine's staff so that the contributions of African-Americans to the history of the United States could be adequately documented. African-American models were used in the magazine's advertisements and a conscious effort was made to portray positive aspects of African-American life and culture. Everything in the magazine was addressed to the African-American consumer. Johnson maintained that Ebony's success was due to the positive image of African Americans that it offered.

In 1951, Johnson launched Tan (a "true confessions" type magazine) and Jet, a weekly news digest. Later publications included African-American Stars and Ebony Jr., a children's magazine. Although all of the magazines achieved a measure of success, none was able to compete with Ebony, which in its 40th year of publication had a circulation of 2,300,000 and was the primary reason that Johnson was considered one of the 400 richest individuals in the United States. Johnson expanded his business interests to areas other than his magazines. He became chairperson and chief executive officer of the Supreme Life Insurance Company. He developed a line of cosmetics, purchased three radio stations, started a book publishing company, a television production company, and served on the board of directors of several major businesses including the Greyhound Corporation.

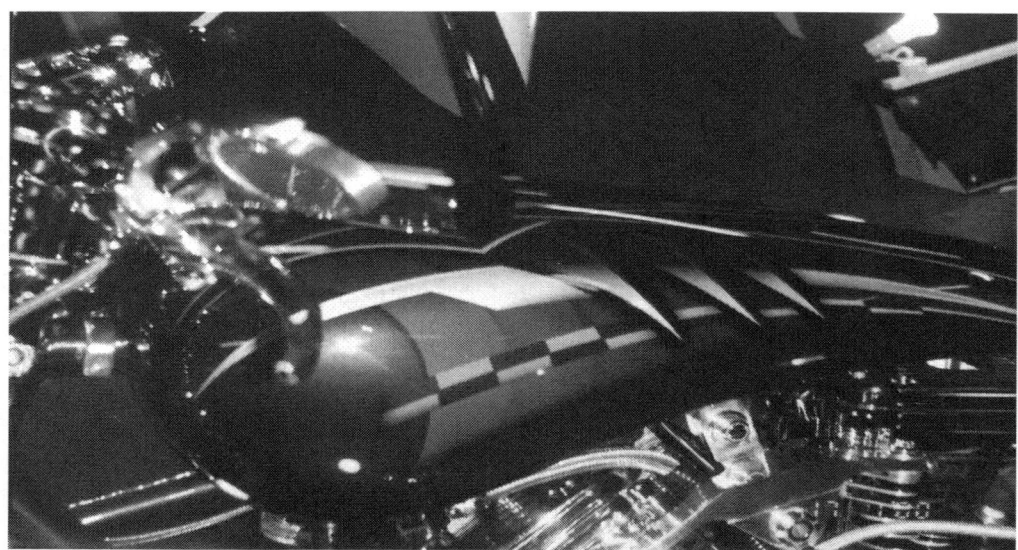

Airbrush art mostly consisted of automotive art, evening sunsets, and name designs prior to Malcolm arriving on the scene.

Vision of Being the Best

I always had a dream to be the best airbrush artist in the world. Not only did I want to be the best I wanted the recognition of being the first African-American artist that has his own airbrush company. My goal was to sell all of the airbrush equipment including; paints, stencils, airbrushes, DVDs and training seminars. From the first time I saw an airbrush being used by an artist I knew that I was going to change the game once I learned how to use this tool.

Malcolm at his first airbrush conference bringing a little "color" to the event.

It was something that fueled me because ever since I could remember I had never seen an airbrush artist of color published in any publications. All the art that I seen created with the airbrush was mostly Florida beach scenes and cute name designs. I wanted to share with the world the urban airbrush art that I was seeing in my community. This drove me to become a researcher and visionary on how I could be the artist that successfully represented the urban airbrush movement.

I knew that I wanted to be the best so I would study the best. I started studying to be the best at my craft when I was a kid. I would go to the library and check out any and every book that had anything to do with an airbrush. Before I knew it I had magazines and articles. I even called up multiple airbrush companies to get their free catalogs. I was studying years before I could even afford an airbrush. I like to think that I knew more about how the airbrush worked before I even held my first one.

I was 16 years old when I heard about some airbrush classes in Las Vegas. I read about some training and I dreamed of going. If I want to be the best I would have to learn from some of the best in the industry. I knew that one day I was going to go and learn but, of course, I didn't have the money to go. I made a pact with myself to go the next year. It cost me $900.00 for the flight and hotel and it took me months to save up the money. The class was another $400.00! I managed to get a big mural project at Gray's Child Care in Milwaukee and that took care of my tuition. It was my first time flying that far away from home by myself. My father encouraged me to go and helped me reserve my seat at the training. Soon I was on an early morning flight to Las Vegas.

I had never been out to Vegas and it was incredible. I was so excited to go and learn. I took a cab to the hotel after I grabbed my bags and arrived at the Golden Nugget. I go to check in and register for the training. As I'm filling out the paper work the lady asks for my drivers license. I politely let her know that I was only 17 and I didn't have my license yet. She gave me a concerning look. She starts to look behind me and around the room. She was looking for my guardian that I must have come with. I reminded her that I'm 17. She was puzzled. She started to ask me questions like, "Who flew you to Las Vegas?" and, "Did you enroll in this training all by yourself?" I said, "Yes."

She called the show manger. She left the registration table and the show manager and she went to the back to talk. I could see them through an opening in the drapery and I could tell that there was a problem. I wasn't suppose to be allowed to be in a hotel Casino without an adult and I had managed to book my hotel room as well. The hotel management was called and they agreed to call my father and put the room in his name.

I was finally there. I remembered all of the dreams that I had at that moment. I'm finally here in Las Vegas learning from the best. The main class that I was so eager to attend was Craig Fraser's Beginner Automotive course. I wanted to learn the foundation of airbrushing on cars, motorcycles and the right way to customize vehicles. I woke up the first day so excited. I still couldn't believe I was there learning from Craig Fraser, one of the premiere airbrush artists in the world.

I learned so much that weekend and that was my first time investing in training and coaching. I realized that I could use this as a tool to speed up my productivity. The vision and desire that I had to be the best pushed me to enroll in the training in Las Vegas. I then knew that I was going to be one the best airbrush artists in the world because with the right vision and focus I can overcome any obstacle.

That weekend started a life decision to travel and learn from the best. I have even invited friends to accompany me but I quickly realized that most people look at traveling and attending a conference or training as an expense and not an opportunity to learn and grow. I always looked at it as an investment. As I began to learn and travel to more conferences and training the more the gurus started to notice me. I started to go to the conferences just to have an opportunity to meet mentors and associate myself with successful people.

Malcolm with a fellow student from California, both of whom attended the airbrush conference in Las Vegas.

As he traveled to more conferences and training the more people started to notice.

He attended conferences to have an opportunity to meet mentors and associate with successful people.

Chapter 3

THE ART OF
SUCCESS #AOSBOOK

www.MalcolmMccrae.com

46

Success Mindset
[sək'ses] [mīn(d)set]

Believe, Overcome, Compete, Study, Focus

       Successful people believe in growth. They believe their skills will improve as they gain experience. They believe they will find road maps, strategies, and resources that will produce the results they want. If we are confident that we will overcome these challenges, we learn from them and keep trying until we find a successful course of action. The traits associated with a growth mindset are a recipe for success. When we choose the growth mindset over the fixed mindset, where you are today becomes irrelevant. The only thing that matters is where we're going.

Nkyinkyim

Five Things You Must Do to Develop a Mindset for Success

1. Believe You'll Succeed
2. Overcome One Obstacle At a Time
3. Only Compete with Yourself
4. Study Great People
5. Focus

Believe You'll Succeed

You evaluate the available options in search of the most promising way forward. You persevere through setbacks because you're certain you will surpass them and continue the journey towards success. People react differently to similar situations based on their beliefs. When faced with adversity, one person understands it's a normal part of the process while another person complains that "things never go right for me" and gives up. The first person cultivated a mental framework that leads to a productive response to the setback. If you believe there's an answer to a challenging problem, you send your brain on a mission to find that answer. You focus on the possibilities and solutions that will drive you forward. On the other hand, if you believe the problem is unsolvable, you direct your brain to find the best excuses available.

Overcome One Obstacle at a Time

When we attach to the outcome, we mentally rush towards the finish line. In this frame of mind, we put tremendous pressure on ourselves to succeed. We obsess over all the obstacles we may face. We don't embrace incremental progress and growth. We want to fast track to the rewards of success. We can't effectively handle ten obstacles at once. Our mind doesn't know where to direct its attention. Our attention scatters and our productive energy dissipates. We can overcome one challenge at a time though. We can methodically analyze each challenge from all angles. Then, we can develop strategies to attack the challenge in the way that's most likely to succeed. We commit to a plan and surge ahead. There's a long journey ahead with many peaks and valleys. Yet, we don't need to find solutions for problems until we face them. Breaking down the goal and focusing solely on the next challenge is achievable. This mindset produces consistent action, which adds up to massive progress over time.

Only Compete with Yourself

Modeling the mindsets, strategies, and actions of those who have already accomplished what we're pursuing is valuable. Through modeling, we avoid some of the mistakes others made on the road to success. We discover a proven blueprint that shortens the time it takes us to reach our goals. While learning from others facilitates our growth, mentally competing with them produces detrimental consequences. When we measure ourselves against others, we look towards more successful people. This leads us to feel inadequate and doubt our ability. When we shift our paradigms and compete only with ourselves, we zoom in on our path. We're not concerned with what everyone else is doing anymore. We're simply trying to improve from where we were yesterday. We're focused on improving our skills and equipping ourselves with the tools we need to achieve our goals. We measure success based on our personal benchmarks instead of how others define success.

Study Great People

Spend some time to find great people in your life to study. Look for traits that are similar to your life. These make it easier to paint the picture in your head of what your success will feel like. There are trails to success. Write these traits down and put them into a list this will help you remember these clues. Most successful people leave paths towards their success. They leave clues if you know what to look for. These clues can be found in books or stories. Most times it's small detailed parts that propelled this person's career. I love to learn about greatness. From sports players like Michael Jordan to jazz musicians that changed the world through their music like Louis Armstrong.

Louis Armstrong (August 4, 1901 – July 6, 1971), nicknamed Satchmo, Satch, or Pops, was an American trumpeter, composer, singer and actor who was one of the most influential figures in jazz. His career spanned five decades, from the 1920s to the 1960s. With his instantly recognizable gravelly voice, Armstrong was an influential singer, demonstrating great dexterity as an improviser. Armstrong was one of the first popular African-American entertainers to "cross over" whose skin color was secondary to his music in an America that was extremely racially divided allowing him socially acceptable access to the upper echelons of American society which were highly restricted for black men of his era. *Wikipedia contributors. "Louis Armstrong." Wikipedia, The Free Encyclopedia. Wikipedia, The Free Encyclopedia, 10 May. 2017. Web. 11 May. 2017.*

(Louis Armstrong) ©WWW.MALCOLMMCCRAE.COM 2012

Focus

Focus is one of many tools in your mental arsenal of success. The ability to focus in on opportunities, projects, business and family is what separates highly successful people from normal people. There will be thousands of distractions, excuses and people who will try to knock you off of your focus. Success is a combination of vision, focus, passion, and action. The successful people know that with these four principles anything is possible. This way of thinking has landed me with some of the most profitable business deals and major growth every year. As I travel the world conducting dozens of talks every year, people always ask me how do I travel the world, create incredible art and run a successful speaking business all while still being an incredible father and husband and family man. My answer is I'm a highly productive and focused individual. I create buffers in my life that filter out time wasting situations and people like; privacy, space, objectives and truth.

This gives me the opportunity to spend my time wisely. Everyday I say to myself "gotta stay focused" over 200 times. This programs my subconscious to not get distracted. As an author I have to stay focused on writing time and reflection time in my life. If I don't have buffers I could never get anything done, especially this book. Success is a journey that can go up, down, right or left. You will always have options on where to go on your path. Some of the options will knock you off your path to your destination and some will be on the route, the choice is always yours to make. With all of the success I've had I still find myself at a four way stop sometimes. Not knowing what direction to go can be a scary feeling sometimes. What always seems to lead me is my inner conversation that is telling me to focus in on the path that will lead me to my success or goals in life.

Please use this book as a map to the treasure which is your success in life. It will not be easy, it may be some of the hardest, most uncomfortable things that you will ever do, but it is worth it. Use these tools I share with you on your journey and stay focused on your path, it will be incredible! The principal of focus is one of the most important principles in this book. Being focused is the key to success as we start the process of following your dreams for success. Being focused is a mindset and that is necessary to be great at anything.

Four Principles I Use in My Life to Help Keep Me Focused

1. Keep Your Vision to Yourself
2. Find a Working Environment
3. Focus In On Your Objective or End Results
4. Find Your "Why" in Everything You Do

Keep Your Vision to Yourself

Keep your ideas and visions to yourself. Stay away from haters, complainers and procrastinators. These people can be dream killers. When you're focused on your vision it's so easy to want to share your thoughts and ideas with friends and family. While working on my passion I realized it was a lonely path. Most of the time I wanted to just find someone that I could share my ideas with. I found out immediately that most people never fulfilled their own dreams. Most people will give bad advice because most times they were not able to stay focused enough to be whatever they dreamed to be.
I had to learn this principle the hard way. I can remember times when I had a exciting idea. The first thing I wanted to do is tell my friend Murphy. Murphy was a good friend, I thought, but every time I would come to him excited about my new ideas I can remember leaving our discussions feeling confused and uninspired. After the third time I started to see a pattern. I would come in excited and positive and I would leave the conversation depressed and defeated. Murphy would tell me all of the difficult issues and problems I would have to go through to make my idea happen. He would always start off with you don't have the money, expertise or people to do it. Followed by "I tried that and it won't work because...." It was my first time that I realized that I have to keep my dreams to myself until I'm ready to ask people for their opinion. The key is to stay focused on doing the work. This is your dream or vision not their's so stop asking or looking for other people's approval. Start the process and ask for critiques during the later parts of the process not during the early stages. Build it in your mind, develop the concept and start the process.

Find a Working Environment

Each year I take two to three weeks off to reboot my energy. I usually do this at the and of the year. I find a special place in my home or office where I can get myself away from distractions and focus in on next years goals accomplishments. This space should be a controlled environment where you can lock out any distractions.

Focus In On Your Objective or End Results

There will be hard times while you are working towards your success. When you find yourself going through a rough spell on your journey take some time to reflect on your end goal or objective. Visualize completing your goal. The feeling of joy and happiness that you will feel once you have accomplished the task will help give you the fuel needed to keep pushing on. This is how I have accomplished some of the most difficult tasks that I have had in my life. For instance, when writing my first book *"To Live, To Create, To Inspire How Art Saved My Life"* I was lost. I had no experience in writing a book, in fact, I was a horrible writer and speller in school. I knew that the odds were against me but I didn't care. I kept thinking to myself how incredible it would be to have a finished book. I visualized the glossy cover and the new book smell. I even visualized the great conversations I would have with the readers. My mind switched from what the problems could be to what the possibilities are. I remember the long nights of typing and editing thinking to myself will I ever get this book complete and out of my head. I would take that frustration and use it as a tool to keep me focused. I would remind myself that I would be letting myself and the world down if I didn't share this information in a book.

Find Your "Why" in Everything You Do

The first time I even heard this term, "What's your why?" was from Dr. Eric Thomas the incredible speaker, author and educator. He describes it as your "why" and is the reason for pushing yourself towards success. It is your inner quest for truth. Your "why" has to be bigger than yourself. It has to be a life mission that will not only be about the amount of money you might make. High achievers use their "why" as a tool. For some people their "why" might be their family or children. For me there has been no greater driving force than my family. My family are the pictures that pop in to my mind when I have an obstacle to overcome. Most times I couldn't do it for myself but when I think about how my family is depending on me it gives me that extra courage to push on. Find your "why."

"I can accept failure,
everyone fails
at something.
But I can't
accept not trying."

-Michael Jordan

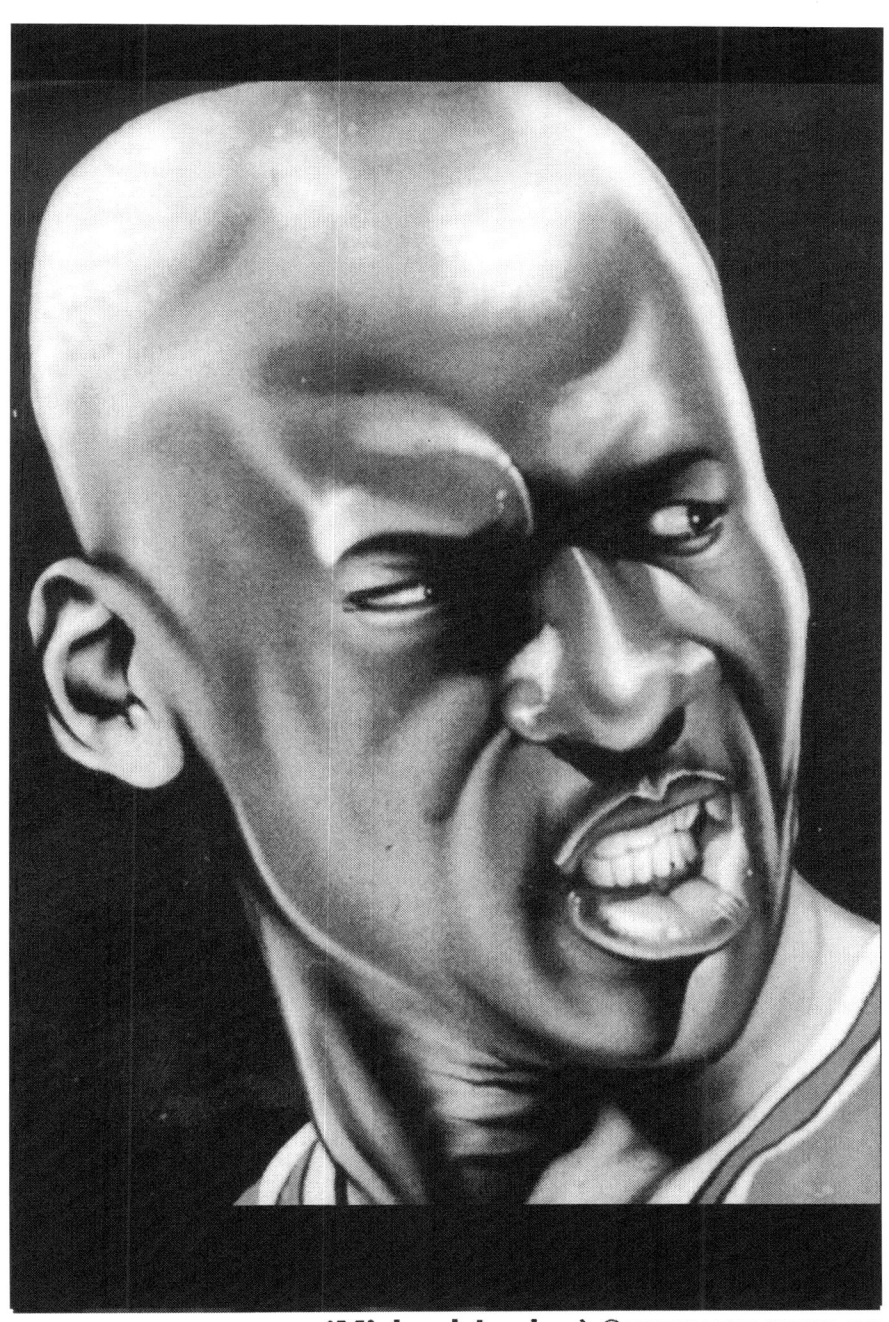

(Michael Jordan) ©WWW.MALCOLMMCCRAE.COM 2012

Chapter 4

THE ART OF SUCCESS #AOSBOOK

www.MalcolmMccrae.com

Value
[valyōo]

A person's principles
or standards of behavior.
One's judgment of
what is important in life.

Nssa

Value - Discover Your Worth

The human body is an electro-chemical machine involving lots of things in the course of its functions. Many of the main body organs operate on an electrical basis. You cannot move a finger without electrical charges being involved. The brain and the heart and other organs continue their work because of electrical charges. Scientists and researchers have calculated that the hydrogen atoms in the human body of one person, if they could be utilized, would supply the electrical needs of a highly productive country like the United States or China for nearly a week. That would be more than eleven million kilowatt hours per body mass. That means that the average person, by this estimate, is worth nearly $85 billion. Knowing your worth is important when it comes to being successful. Most high achievers understand that how you think about yourself is more important than what people think of you. How you feel about yourself impacts virtually every aspect of our lives. Our personal value system is not based on what society thinks of you it is solely based on your personal goals and ambitions in life. It's part of your self image.

"I was forced to be an artist and a CEO from the beginning, so I was forced to be like a businessman because when I was trying to get a record deal, it was so hard to get a record deal on my own that it was either give up or create my own company."

-Jay-Z

(Jay-Z) ©WWW.MALCOLMMCCRAE.COM 2012

Value - The Starving Artist Mentality
(Must read for any creative person who wants to be successful)

I started to see this at an early age. The first time I can remember is when I was in high school. I attended The Milwaukee High School for the Arts. That's where I started to hang and socialize with other creatives. I immediately realized that I was different from most young creative youth. I loved creating but I always looked at my talent as a way to make a living or at least make some cash to get new sneakers.

Since I grew up around entrepreneurs, I always had a mind state that my creations could be sold. Most of my peers were creating just for the sake of creating and most times my school art projects would be prototypes of a new art process that I was going to use for clients. I started to notice that as creatives, we have normal responsibilities like everyone else; the difference is that we create what consumers buy. Think about it. A creative person had a hand in everything that we purchase as consumers. From toothbrushes to clothing; even the car we drive. We don't think about the process or even the value of creativity. The starving artist thinks one-dimensional. He or she looks at their art or service as not having monetary value. Most people don't believe enough in their talent to share it with the world let alone try to sell it. In the art world there is a belief that there is something wrong with making money from your talent or art form. Some say that it takes away from the art as an organic process.

I'm here to tell you that it is a waste of time and talent if you don't make the attempt to make cash from your calling. I see so many creative thinkers who have talent and skill but have the wrong attitude. The key is education. You have to take the initiative to learn the formulas for success. The aspect of a starving artist comes from the lack of nutritional intake. We digest gobs of artistic criticism and opinions of our work, but fail to search or make an attempt to find the nutrition we need that will keep us fed for a lifetime.

This book was written out of the frustration of seeing the world's most creative people unhappy and broke. You must force yourself to change and adapt accordingly. With the Internet we, for the first time in history, as artists and creative people can create, promote and profit off of our talent without the worry of being exploited. My quest is to feed the starving artist with resources and opportunities to grow and build without compromising the art and integrity.

If I Sell It Cheap They Will Buy

A solution to the problem that most artists have with lack of sales is to sell their creations cheap. This outlook is not the correct solution. What that does is depreciate not only the value of your work but the work of other artists in your same genre. Here is an example. When I had my airbrush and screen-printing shop in Milwaukee there were four to five other airbrush shops in the area. There was a lot of competition. One guy decided to sell his airbrush clothing cheaper than anyone in the city. He was like 20% cheaper than anyone else. I get a call from another shop owner worried about losing so much business. He asked if I was going to drop my prices I said,"No." He immediately started telling me how he was going to drop his prices by 30%. I started looking. These guys were price slashing all of their airbrush t-shirts! As the prices got lower the art got sloppier. I, on the other hand maintained my prices.

"It's a waste of time and talent if you don't cash in from your calling."
-Malcolm McCrae

A few months later the guy called me back and asked how business was doing, I said, "Great." He said business for him was so bad that he was thinking about closing his store. He had slashed his prices so low that he wasn't making any money off of his work and his clientele wanted even cheaper prices. He asked me how did I stay afloat while they were killing each other's businesses. I told him that while you guys were cutting your prices and lowering your quality I was building my value and increasing my quality. I knew that the consumer would look at your business as cheap and most would look at something that is too cheap as being inferior. My plan of action was to build on how we were the best at quality, consistency and creativity. A few weeks later three of the five shops were out of business.

Seven Things Successful People Never Waste Time Doing

1. Productive, successful people don't get sucked into social media

2. Productive, successful people don't go through the day without a plan or schedule

3. Productive, successful people don't allow others to waste their time

4. Productive, successful people don't worry about things they can't control

5. Productive, successful people don't hang out with negative people

6. Productive, successful people don't dwell on past mistakes

7. Productive, successful people don't focus on what other people are doing

Time Is Money

Don't waste time. Time is important because it is scarce. When things are scarce, they become valuable because people can't get enough to satisfy their needs. Since no one can reclaim lost time, it's important to make the most of the time one has.

"Time is money," was a phrase used by Benjamin Franklin. This is a term that I use daily in my life. Success is a time sensitive process. It takes decades to learn how to apply these principles. Once you realize how important time is you can understand how achievers use time as a tool. You must create methods in your life that help track your progress. One of my keys to success is using speed and action to get things done. I don't wait on anything if I have an idea about something I move on it. Time and movement work together to create results.

You must understand that we all get 24 hours in a day. Your success is dependent on how you use those hours. As my success grew, I realized that my time management must grow as well. As a professional artist I paint large murals for corporations all over the world. I just finished a large 30 foot installation for a technology company. The company presented me with some ideas of the mural that they wanted me to paint. Next, they wanted a quote on the scope of work. Most artists or interior design firms charge by the square foot; I take a different approach. I charge by the time, labor and materials. Time is the most valuable part of my creative business. It's one of the main tools I use to build value in my craft and company. It's the difference between a $2,000.00 mural project or $20,000.00 mural project. My perspective has never changed about the value of time. Please take some time to think about how you spend your 24 hours.

When you are young you view time differently. You feel that you have all the time in the world. As you get older you realize that time moves fast. I remember when my daughter was three years old and now she is 15 years old. I was just taking here to the circus and now she is a freshman in High School. Time doesn't wait for anyone, not even fathers.

Don't Let Others Determine Your Value

If you don't know your value other people will determine it for you. I live by this slogan everyday. As I write this passage I cant help but to reflect on a business deal that I had been working on for six months. This deal was with a multi-million dollar company. The company had been watching me for years before they contacted me. It was a license deal to produce a line of art materials that would totally change the game. I looked at all of the young people that the products would inspire and motivate. My main goal was to get these products in stores all across the world. Especially stores in areas where young creatives will be. I remember as a kid going into art stores and never seeing any products that looked like the art I wanted to produce. I always looked for paints, airbrushes and even magazines that produced art that represented my culture.

I thought this dream had come true once this company contacted me. One of the things that I've learned in my career is to create the opportunities that I want in life. So I was prepared to deal with this kind of business. I made plans to go visit the corporate headquarters on the east coast once I talked to the executive via phone. I like to do business in person. I like to shake the hands and talk business face-to-face. This has always been my strategy. People act different when you're sitting in the same room together. I'm a detail oriented person. I steady the details of every business move I make. Most of the time the devil is in the details. So I listened and watched as he began to tell me what he thought I wanted to hear.

Always listen when people are talking to you about what you are doing. If you slow down and listen really carefully to people they will always tell you who they really are and what their intentions might be. Pay attention to there body language and how they say things. I listened to what he was saying and it sounded like we could work something out to do business together. We talked about distribution and the overall process and approach of how we would roll out the line of supplies.

I've dealt with a lot of corporations and have done a lot of business deals. One of the things that I watch for when I'm doing business are like minded people or situations that go along with my vision. As I become more successful I become more aware that finding people that have the same vision is the key. Sometimes you have to be prepared to fight for what you believe in. In the case of this business deal the product line was great but the way they were going to market it was not. They showed me the prototype of the first product. It was horrible and overly commercial. Not a representation of who I am or what my brand represents.

I realized that the problem was that this company didn't have the same business values as me. What was important to me, was the feeling of a kid going to the art store and seeing a product that was produced by someone that looked like them. My goal is to be the first African-American airbrush artist to have major distribution in art stores all over the world. What's important to me is to be a tool to inspire more artists. I believe that people buy from the heart especially if it can change lives.

Malcolm realized his dream of being the first African-American airbrush artist to have major distribution in art stores all over the world with "The Assassin" airbrush.

I had to step back and realize my true value. I knew that as bad as I wanted to close this deal that if I just thought about the money that my vision and 15 year journey would be compromised. I decided to call the deal off and the conversation that kept playing in my mind is the conversation that I had with my mentor Eric Thomas.

"When you want to succeed as bad as you want to breathe, then you'll be successful."

-Eric Thomas

Malcolm in Scottsdale, AZ with "The Hip-Hop Preacher" Eric Thomas.

Thomas is a motivational speaker, author and minister. Thomas, born in Chicago, IL, grew up in Detroit, MI. where he dropped out of high school and lived homeless on the streets of for two years. While homeless, he met a preacher who inspired him to go back to school and eventually change lives. Thomas, now a Ph.D. , founded a company to offer education consulting, executive coaching and athletic development. Thomas has given motivational talks to business executives, collegiate and professional athletes. Lebron James credited Thomas as part of his inspiration for winning the 2012 NBA Championship. *Wikipedia contributors. "Eric Thomas (motivational speaker)." Wikipedia, The Free Encyclopedia. Wikipedia, The Free Encyclopedia, 7 May. 2017. Web. 11 May. 2017*

Chapter 5

THE ART OF SUCCESS #AOSBOOK

www.MalcolmMccrae.com

Mentorship

[ˈmentôrSHip, ˈmentərSHip]

The guidance provided by a coach,
mentor or guru.

Boa me na me boa wo

I have had numerous coaches and mentors in my life. This tool has been instrumental in my success and has been one of my secret weapons to personal success. I took advantage of this principle early in my career. I've always had people in my life that have been great counselors. These are people I can call on when I have a problem or just need a bit of advice. Some of my mentors and coaches I have hired and some have came into my life naturally. I can remember always being eager to learn and get better at any task. So I always kept my eye on people that knew more than me. The people in my life that I consider mentors have helped me shape my success.

I now coach and mentor a selected group of people from professional musicians to entrepreneurs and educators across the world. I take great responsibility and honor when I work with a coaching client. I love the process of helping other determined people find their goals to success. I'm very critical on who I teach because it takes an open vessel to learn new things. You can lead the horse to water but you can't make them drink.

I often get asked the question of how do you find a mentor?

Malcolm with mentor Chike Akua Award-Winning Educator, Author and Speaker.

Four Easy Steps to Approaching a Mentor

1. Be clear about what you want

Don't waste your time or the mentors time by telling your whole life story. Be prepared to articulate what you want and how they can best help you.

2. Ask yourself first how do you serve them

Most busy people are up to their neck with people who want there attention. Most have barriers that they have created to discourage any beggars. Most people they encounter want something and have a "hand out" attitude. Your approach must be service driven. You start by giving value and they will pay attention.

3. Write a letter of appreciation of their work

Don't just invest in their books and courses. You must digest their process. You never know when you will be asked to talk about their work. Do not send an email if you can help it. Find their office address and type or hand write a letter. A hand written letter is more personal and makes you stand out. It's all about creating a personal relationship and going the extra mile.

4. Be consistent with follow ups

The money is in the follow up. Take some time calling or reaching out to your potential mentor. The key is not to just check in to see if they received the letter you sent. This step can be done via email if you choose.

Most successful people don't mind sharing their principles of success. The key is to be respectful. The worst thing you can do is ask for funding for your dream. Most people think that all they need to do is meet "X person" and they will get them to fund their business or idea. You are not looking for a fish, you are looking how to be taught to fish. Never go to a successful person and ask for money or a business loan. This is the number one turn off. You have to remember that they receive hundreds of letters from people asking them for money. What makes you different?

Great mentors are people that live by example in all parts of their life. We all have coaches and mentors. These are people that we can call upon for support and counsel. My first mentors were my father and mother. They always inspired me to be great and do my best. A mentor can be a family member or maybe a teacher. In my case I was inspired by many mentors growing up and even to this day I call upon some of my lifelong mentors for guidance and advice. Through my success I have been on a quest for knowledge and have always been a person that enjoys sharing knowledge with people who can use it. I call it the "ah ha" moment. It's when the tools I shared made sense and that person really understood the lesson. I'm so inspired when I see that moment.

I started teaching and mentoring when I opened my first company Sho' Time Wild Image. It all started when a friend of mine stopped in to my business one afternoon. I was right in the middle of painting a pair of custom shoes. One of our specialties was airbrushing high-end sneakers. We had clients that would pay up to $300.00 to get their Jordans or Nikes customized. Business was booming and I had one client drop off 15 pair of shoes. I was swamped with orders. A friend saw my dilemma and offered to send his little brother who was about 14 to help. He went on to explain that his little brother Edward was always drawing and would be great at airbrushing. I really didn't have the time to teach anyone, but I needed the help and thought maybe I could teach him some prepping techniques that would speed up the process. I told him to send his little brother by after he got out of school.

The next day at 3:35 p.m. this skinny kid with braids comes in and introduces himself. "Hi my name is Edward Gordon but my friends call me Doody. My brother Mark said you were looking for help." I looked at this kid and thought what am I going to do with him. I started him off by cleaning the shop. Later I showed him the foundation of how the store is setup. He was a fast learner and listened to the details. I've had some help before from some of the neighborhood kids, but for most of them it was some money to spend at the corner store. Many never took it seriously. I've always had friends that would come help a bit if I call on them but they never really took a real interest in my craft. I gave Doody basic instructions on the proper way to mask sneakers and he listened. I couldn't believe how much work we had gotten done. It was the end of the day and I began to pay Doody for the days work. He counted his money and asked if he could come back tomorrow. I said, "Of course", and that led to a long relationship.

Doody became the first student that I had mentored and taught my craft of airbrushing. He became the lead artist in my company. Doody and I worked well together and started to have great conversations about life. He was now a freshman in high school and started asking me about life issues. I found myself giving him advice about staying focused as a creative person.

The area where the shop was located was in the heart of the north side of Milwaukee and was one of the roughest, poorest areas in the city. Doody lived a couple blocks away from the shop. I immediately noticed that Doody was facing issues from the peer pressure in the streets. Drugs and gangs ran rampant in this area and I saw a lot of the youth around the shop were getting wrapped up with negative things. The homicide rate was at an all time high and the summer was coming up. Most teens of his age where not going to survive the summer. Not without going to jail or getting shot.

I made up my mind that I was going to be a mentor for Doody. Little did I know that there would be numerous other young people that would need my guidance as well. Immediately after I started to let Doody work with me some of his cousins needed jobs and wanted to work at the shop. Before I knew it we had a crew of young men from the ages of 14-18 that were helping run the shop. I began to create bonds with all of these young guys. One of the things I would do is have group meeting where we all could voice our opinions. This gave everyone an opportunity to share their thoughts. Each one of them had their own issues and problems that they were dealing with. I had to learn what it meant to be a great mentor and coach in these young men's lives. I even helped Doody go to prom.

Edward "Doody" Gordon working at the Sho' Time Wild Image. Doody became the first student Malcolm mentored and taught the craft of airbrushing. He later became the lead artist at the company. Now Doody owns his own airbrush company.

As a mentor in their lives I was able to help them cope with life issues. I remember one day when I was working late and heard a knock at the door. We had so many young people that everyday I would get mothers begging me to mentor their son or daughter. There are only so many work hours in a day. We would allow some of the youth to come work for a couple of hours just to stay out of the streets. Sometimes they didn't even want to get paid. They just wanted to be apart of Sho' Time Wild Image and have the opportunity to be a part of our "apprentice program." This need eventually turned into a community grassroots mentorship and apprenticeship opportunity for young people. The word was getting out and the young people started to come. My father Pops was teaching a group of them how to screen print and prep for T-Shirt orders.

One day this kid comes in. He explains that he is homeless and from Gary, Indiana. I was appalled. He had a garbage bag with his clothes and barely knew anyone in Milwaukee. I could tell he hadn't taken a shower in days and he was hungry. A couple of blocks away from the shop was a Boys & Girls Club on 34th North Avenue. My dad trained a faculty member at the Boys & Girls Club and they opened a screen printing shop at the location. The kid said he had attended the club and they were looking for help and that they had showed him how to screen print shirts. He was on his last straw and was about to sell some dope or rob somebody to get something to eat. I looked in his eyes and saw a desperate and afraid kid but others would have seen a criminal. He was really rough around the edges. He never smiled or grinned. He was tough and didn't take no mess.

When I started working with young people I created a rule that if they come and they really wanted it then they deserved a chance. I gave him his chance and he became part of the family. He became a leader in the shop with his no nonsense approach. He immediately showed potential and I made him my screen printing production manager. Eventually he oversaw all of the screen printing orders making sure that everything was prepared. Pops would ultimately train him to be a master screen printer.

One of the youngest students I hired and mentored was 14. His name was Lee. This young man was brought to me by a friend of mine, DeVon Dent. He was his little cousin. DeVon told me about his little cousin, Lee, who was designing and creating his own video games. His mother brought Lee to the shop and he had his portfolio with him. He had incredible talent with the computer and vision to create anything that he put his mind to. He explained to me that he was self-taught and would spend hours in his room teaching himself on the newest programs such as Corel Draw and Adobe Photoshop.

It was great timing as I had just updated our graphic design department. I had just purchased over $5000.00 in computers, Epson printers and a vinyl plotter. The problem I ran into was I didn't know how to use any of the programs and didn't have much time to learn because business was booming. I taught myself the basics so I brought Lee in to see what he could do. He immediately took over the space and he became the lead graphic designer for our shop. He designed all of the screen printing films that were needed to create the screens. Lee was responsible for over 200 layouts a month at the height of the shop. He became one of the most talented and driven young creatives that I had a pleasure mentoring.

Interior shot of Sho' Time Wild Image, Malcolm's first shop in Milwaukee, WI.

Ten Rules for Mentorship

1. Never abuse your power
2. Respect your students
3. Only teach what you know best
4. Push yourself and your mentees
5. Create tools
6. Expect results
7. Lead by example
8. Choose your students wisely
9. Continue to study
10. Reward growth

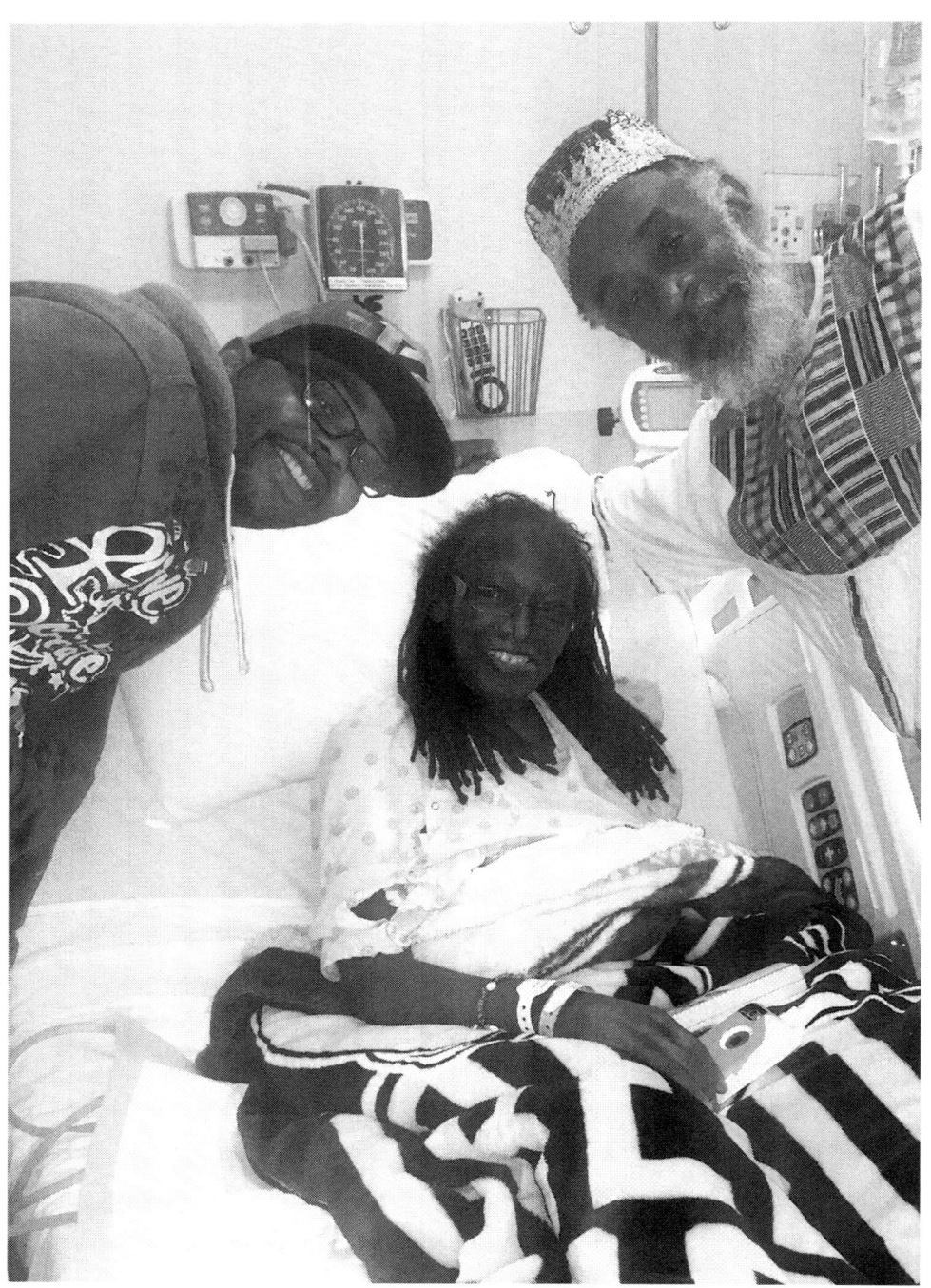

Malcolm and Pops with mentor Redonna Rodgers founder of The Center for Teaching Entrepreneurship in Milwaukee, WI.

Being of service. I love this model. "The game should be sold... not told." In a nut shell this explains that nothing is free. Even knowledge costs money. Time is money. If someone takes the time to teach you something be grateful. I've been a master at learning from someone else's mistakes. I listen and watch other people make mistakes and make mental notes to myself to remind me what not to do. This way of thinking is important. Always ask your mentors about stories of when they had to push or fight for their success. These stories become tools that you can use as references in your life. Listen to the good and the bad. The bad is my favorite part because I get more out of the struggle then the good times which will take care of themselves. It's the bad times that build character, courage and determination.

In my life I've been honored to be a fly on the wall. There have been situations where the best thing for me to do is watch and learn. My gurus and coaches help me to listen and observe more. Sometimes you can't see the full picture because you are in the frame. These people help you see things from other angles. I travel a couple times a year to visit my mentors and coaches in person. There is always a new lesson to learn or something you could add in your life to increase your success.

A great mentor sharpens your skill. Like the saying, "Steel sharpens steel." This is why it is so important to make sure that both parties are able to work together. If there isn't a mutual understanding then the marriage will not work.

"A great mentor sharpens your skill."
- Malcolm McCrae

Chapter 6

THE ART
SUCCESS #AOSBOOK

www.MalcolmMccrae.com

Courage
[kərij]

The ability to do something
that frightens one.
Strength in the face of pain or grief.

Tabon

"Opportunity often comes disguised in the form of misfortune, or temporary defeat."

-Napoleon Hill

(COURAGE) ©WWW.MALCOLMMCCRAE.COM 2015

Courage - Overcoming Adversity

I hear people say all the time that they stay in their "own lane." To be really successful in business you have to create your own lane. Let's look at hip hop for instance. Take someone like Russell Simmons. I recently read one of his books. He said he was doing great with Def Jam as a rap label, but he started to notice these clothing companies like Cross Color and Karl Kani. The youth wore this fashion and they were becoming clothing lines that represented hip hop culture. So Russell Simmons decided he would start his own line called Phat Farm. Russell says in his book everyone thought he was crazy. His business partners were laughing at him and his accountant told him he would go broke if he kept putting money into this idea. Russell says that he lost money for six years and put 10 million dollars in cash into his vision of Phat Farm.

Russell Simmons is an entrepreneur, producer and author. The Chairman and CEO of Rush Communications, he cofounded the hip-hop music label Def Jam Recordings and created the clothing fashion lines Phat Farm, Argyleculture, and Tantris.

Phat Farm is a hip-hop clothing brand created by Russell Simmons. Def Jam label rappers like Ludacris, Redman and DMX had a contract to wear this brand in their various clips to promote the brand.

But he believed in his dream and kept on pushing. People were telling him to stick to music and stay in his lane. But sometimes you have to create your own lane. In 2009 New York Times reported that Russell Simmons sold the Phat Farm brand for $140 million, plus performance incentives. He sold the company to Kellwood, one of the country's largest clothing producers. That's just one story of how creating your own path and being versatile in the marketplace can pay off.

Courage - Don't Take "No" for an Answer

As I look back at my life I reflect on people who taught me lessons. My father was an entrepreneur and hung around other entrepreneurs and they gave me guidance as I was growing up. I worked for some of them during the summer months. One particular friend of my father's was a man named Andre A.K.A. Dre. He was a businessman from Chicago, Illinois. He had hustle and could sell anything. He could sell water to a well. One summer I had an opportunity to work with Andre. My brother Doobie and I would be picked up early in the morning in his cargo van. Andre would travel around to businesses selling different merchandise from T-shirts to incense sticks; even little girl's hair barrettes.

I was so amazed by Andre. He was the true definition of an entrepreneur. He would take us around on a weekly routine of laundromats, barbershops and even hairdressing shops, anywhere where people had cash. I dreaded laundromats, they were always hot. A lot of times people seemed like they didn't want to be bothered and I always got a lot of change. Of course Andre being a businessman didn't care - nickels, quarters, dimes, pennies - it was all money to him. Our normal route included at least two to three laundromats per day. So the spiel would go, "Hey, good morning (or good afternoon), I wanted to see if you would be interested in any of my incredible deals on T-shirts, I even have barrettes." Barrettes were the number one seller. Everyone wanted to make sure that they're little girl's hair was looking cute.

My favorite places to go sell the barrettes were barbershops and hair salons. I loved these places because it was a fast paced market and if you had great service you normally could make great sales. The number one thing was to be able to pre-plan and have everything organized in your duffel bag. So I would come in and go directly to the first guy that I saw. Service is the best tool. As he sat down comfortably and let the barber shave him, I start pulling out the merchandise from the bag and started displaying it in my hands. Then I began to do my pitch, "T-shirts, hats, sweatshirts. Low, low prices!! Buy one, get one free, half off." I walked from barber stand to barber stand, and the customers started to ask questions. The more they asked questions the more I engaged letting them know I had all sizes. Then I would get a bite. The customer would stand up out of the chair, feel the garment and go into his pocket to bring out a $50 bill. They would say, "You got change for a $50 little man?" The sweater was $25, so I didn't mind making change for $50.

My goal was always to get one person to buy and then start a buying frenzy. This is a technique that I learned from Dre. Most times people want to buy but are scared to be the first one. So when you have someone that breaks the ice you can just play off of that and keep the crowd going by playing off of that energy. We had our peaks and we had our lows too. One of the main things that we always dreaded was going up to someone and hearing the word "no." Sometimes there were days when no one wanted to buy. One of the things that Andre taught me is no doesn't mean no. Don't take "no" for an answer.

Don't take the word no personal. When someone doesn't want to buy just move on to the next person until you get a yes. This was a process that I needed to learn. When I first started off I was a bit shy and scared that I wasn't going to be able to make a sale. But immediately after trying I made my first sale, it was incredible! It immediately boosted my confidence and I began to understand this idea of not taking the word no personal. I have built many businesses and have had many ideas. I still to this day use the word no as a tool to push me towards greatness.

"We must build dikes of courage to hold back the flood of fear."
-Martin Luther King, Jr.

In this day and age creative people have to create their own financial success through quality business products and services. Invest in yourself. The number one thing that separates successful people from normal people is hard work and commitment. Every year millions of people make New Year's resolutions to do something new or different from what they did the previous year. For some, it's to stop smoking. For others, it's working out and better health. For me, it was changing my mindset from a poverty mindset to a prosperity mindset.

For example, take when I was working on my first book. I wanted to have this book completed by March 22, 2013. The reason that the date was so important was because that weekend was the National Arts and Education Conference in Fort Worth, TX. So when I began it was October 2012 that gave me six months to write it, find a publisher and promote it. First of all let me make this clear; I had never written a book and failed English in school. So here I am trying to figure this process out, but I made a commitment to myself, so I wouldn't back out. I started to promote the book with a release date of March. Not only did I just promote it, I started selling preorders via Facebook and my website. Now this would force and push me to get this book complete because I used the pressure of the preorders to keep me focused. I worked and worked, writing, organizing and editing, submitting it to publishers all across the country. By January I had a strong final draft complete. I found a publisher that would publish the book for me. So I was right on time. The book was published and I made it to Forth Worth, TX to debut the book. I've used this process of pressure and self-commitment to produce many of my products and services. This method can be applied to any project or goal that you want to accomplish.

"As you start building your dream to change the world, you become the dream that changes the world."
-Malcolm McCrae

"Malcolm McCrae is truly a master of his craft whose expertise has been forged in the fiery streets of urban America. His book is a must-read for educators who understand that we must tap into the multiple intelligences to release the academic and creative genius of our students."
-Chike Akua,
Award-Winning Educator & Author

Five Ways To Overcome Adversity

1.Have the Right Mindset

2. Stop Making Excuses

3.Have Faith

4. Don't Take "No" for An Answer

5. Don't Make Decisions Out of
   F.E.A.R.

Have the right mindset

Your thoughts are essential; they frame the triumphs or tragedies of your life.

Stop making excuses

Excuses are the lies we tell ourselves when we're too afraid of the future.

Have faith

How many times have you heard it said, "Believe you can do it and you can! In history great many tales and stories have been told about the power produced by having faith. Men and women have been able to overcome obstacles and accomplish amazing things by believing in a calling that is bigger than themselves. Maintaining ones faith is a strong act of believing. Faith generates action that leads great people to succeed.

Don't take "no" for an answer.

Need I say more?

Don't make decisions out of F.E.A.R.

False
Expectations
Appearing
Real

No one is immune from failure. Everyone is afraid of something during their lifetime. The thing to remember is that fear is an emotion. The key is learning how to control the way your mind processes the emotion of fear. Fear affects people in one of two ways. It can be used to challenge an individual to be greater, or it can discourage one from trying again. Most people give up and quit at the first sign of adversity, even before it overtakes them.

"I'm always making a comeback but nobody ever tells me where I've been."

-Billie Holiday

(Billy Cry) ©Malcolm McCrae 2012

Chapter 7

THE ART
SUCCESS #AOSBOOK

www.MalcolmMccrae.com

Goals and Objectives

Goal
[gōl//]
Outcome that a person or a system envisions, plans and commits to achieve.

Objectives
[Əbˈjektiv]
Strategies or implementation steps to attain the identified goals. Unlike goals, objectives are specific, measurable, and have a defined completion date.

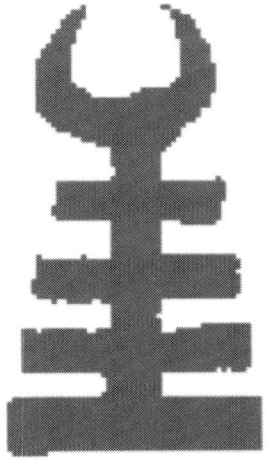

Akoben

Goals and Objectives

Goals give you a reason to work hard. We are so used to accomplishing things in our lives because of obligation. So what we have to do is take that mindset and use it to accomplish personal obligations. Goals keep you focused. For example, in 2010 my home and business got flooded in one of the worst floods in the last century in Southern Missouri. I was devastated. I woke up to a phone call from my neighbor across the street. He was asking if my house had water coming in but I was still in bed. Keep in mind that my bedroom was on the second floor so I said no, my house isn't flooding. As I'm talking I go downstairs and see furniture floating. I had just purchased a brand new air conditioner the day before and left it on the floor near the front door. As I glance across the room I see the A/C floating in a corner almost fully submerged in water. Before I could I call my neighbor back and explain the situation he calls me back telling me that the National Guard was executing an immediate evacuation. I threw some clothes on, grabbed some things and tossed them in my truck and positioned all of my electronics and valuables upstairs.

Any disruption to your life can be difficult. In 2010, Malcolm's home and business was flooded in one of the worst floods in Southeast Missouri in 100 years. One of Malcolm's mentors gave him a sage piece of advice as the reality set in, "Sweep!"

I evacuated and left for two weeks to stay with a friend. Two weeks later I returned to my property to see nothing but devastation. Things were molding. There was no running water and all of my furniture was destroyed. All of the floors were buckled and cracked. The only area that was somewhat undamaged was the floor in my warehouse because it was concrete. My spirit was broken. A day went by and I made up my mind that I was going to start the cleaning process. I wrote down a list of goals and objectives that I needed to complete. The list included demolition, power washing and trashing things. But there was so much stuff I couldn't figure out what to do first. I called a great mentor and friend of mine and started to explain to him my frustrated situation. I went on and on explaining to him what happened. He said one word, "sweep." I was thrown off by his response. He said start off by sweeping the floor and when you start the process of sweeping the floor you will be forced to do the next task.

That next task will take you into your list of goals. See, sometimes we have to just get started and that momentum will push us to accomplish one goal at a time. I realized that I was focusing so much energy on the chaos that I couldn't find a beginning or starting point towards the clean up. Start your goal and objective list today so you can start sweeping up your life. Fear plays a role in a lot of the decisions we make. I'm always trying to make sure I don't make decisions out of fear. Fear is associated with the feeling of failure or doubt. Next time you encounter failure, remember that every failure carries within it the seed of an incredible benefit. Your dreams and ideas are but a seed that has to be planted by action. You may ask yourself what determines a person's failure.

Be Patient and Don't Rush the Process

As we start to move forward and work on this thing called success we must prepare ourselves. The end result is important but the most important thing that most people overlook is the process. The process is what is done everyday; the process involves continuous practice. This is what sustains you through the slow times. When you have a daily practice it keeps your head and actions focused on the hard work. The hard work is what builds greatness. Not only hard work when it's time to produce but hard work in everything that leads up to accomplishing the goal. You can never be successful until you develop an overview of what success means to you.

We all want great lives, more money, a better car, etc. But if I ask you how much more money do you want this week, month, or year most of us would have to think about it. If I ask you to describe what your success looks like - not your neighbor's success or a friends' success but your success - would you know? I want a full HD view of what your life would be if you had this thing called success. One of the most important practices that I have applied almost daily in my life is writing down my goals and plans. These are tasks that are short term and long term. Things that I can accomplish that day, that week, or that month. After I write these things out I then begin to categorize them by time and urgency. I number them from 1 to 10; 1 being the most important and 10 being less urgent. This practice helps all of your ideas, thoughts and plans to get out of your head where they get forgotten and jumbled. This is a practice of clearing your head and starting the process of building your road map.

Create a Goal Board

A goal board is a tool used to get your ideas or visions out of your mind. This board can be as large as you want it. You can use a standard dry eraser board. I have even purchased the white board paint and made a whole wall dry erasable. Write your goals or projects out as clear as possible. Don't think about spelling or any problems that may be an obstacle while fulfilling your goal. Just write all of the ideas out. It's the first step to bringing any goal to reality. Use this board as a tool to stay focused. Now start numbering them. One being the most important thing that will help you succeed and the last being things that might be less important. What you are doing is mentally organizing your thoughts and systematically focusing on what's the most important goal that will lead you to your ultimate success faster.

Liability or Asset?

I was on the road traveling across the country selling airbrush t-shirts, hats and other customizable products when something happened. I started to look at the other vendors. Most of these people were road vets. They traveled the country and even the world touring with a promoter. These vendors were based all over the United States. They would meet up in different cities to sell their products at these "Liquidation Sales." Some of these people were on the road for months and even years traveling from state to state. Their bodies

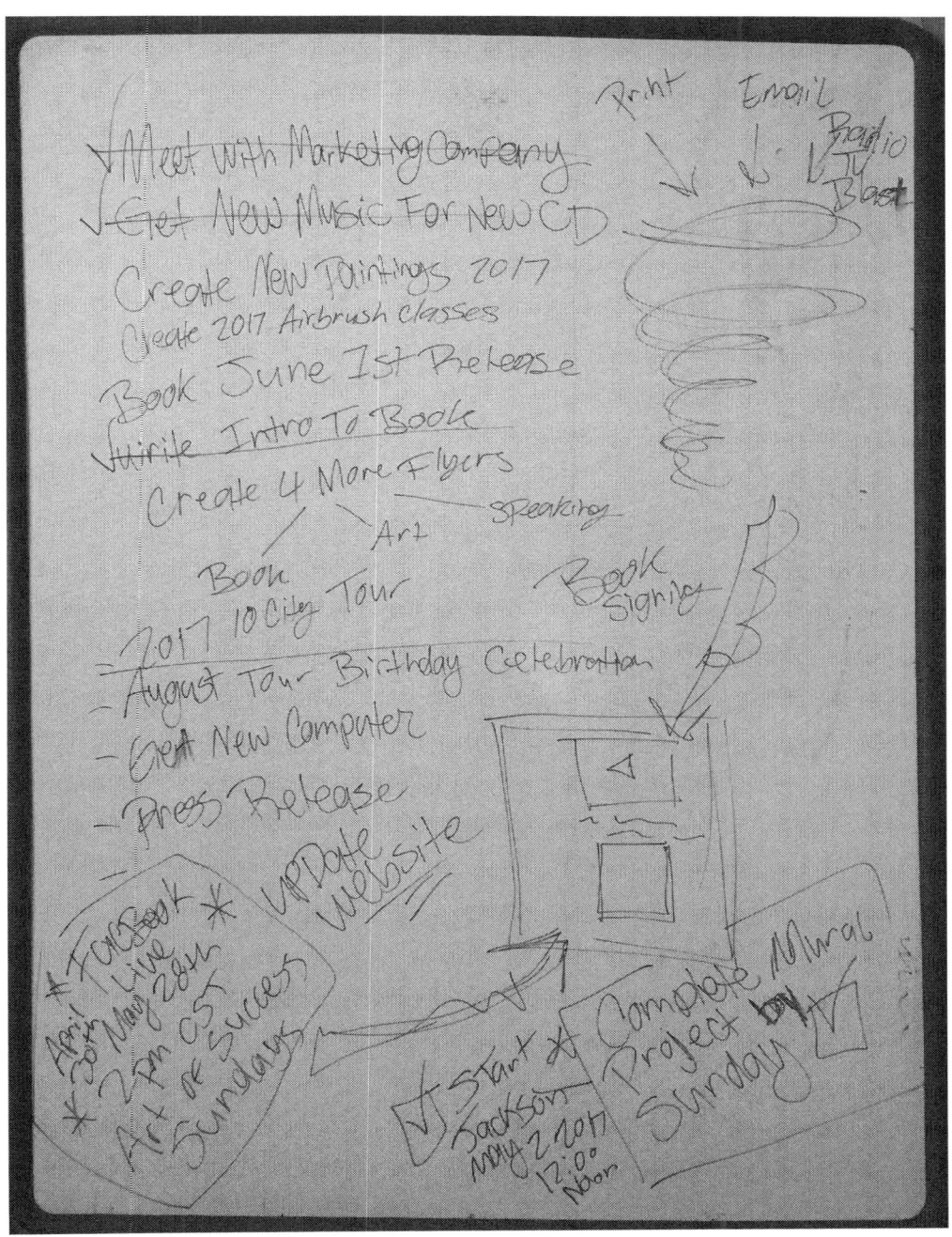

One of Malcolm's many goal boards. A goal board is a tool used to get your vision, goals and ideas out. This board can be as large as you need it to be. Use your board as a tool to stay focused and on track. When creating your goals make sure you start off by writing every idea and goal out. Write it out so it's out of your head. That's the first step to bringing it to reality.

were broken down from the years of eating unhealthy, fast foods and they all had back problems from driving and working long hours on their feet. Most were men but there were women entrepreneurs as well. They all loved the chase and the thrill of the money. I would guess most were in their late 40's. I looked at them but I didn't see that for my future. I was around 25 years-old and knew I had to find a better way to live. Time seems to move fast when you're on the road and I had seen how these people had become slaves to their own businesses. I was tired of Milwaukee and I hated the cold weather. I was on the road for so long that Milwaukee was only a base for me. I knew in my heart that it was time to go. I had numerous employees that I had working on the road for me and the business was growing.

Remember my good friend, DeVon from Chapter Five? One day he was talking with me about choices. At the time DeVon was a record executive. 3D entertainment was the name of his record company and he was the head engineer at a million dollar recording studio that was located on the south side of Milwaukee. DeVon recorded some of the hottest hip-hop and R&B artists at the time. He was locally respected and nationally known. He was explaining to me the difference between a liability or asset and how this way of thinking was critical in life. He went on to say how success is based on two principles. Liability; something that is not reliable or accountable. It brings no value and only takes value away. Or a an asset; a useful or valuable thing, person, or quality. I didn't quite understand what that had to do with success or even life.

He described how one has to be careful not to invest in people or things that can be a liability in life. We must always question the people around us making sure that these people are not takers and power suckers. In life it's all about balance and we all must give and take evenly. Everyone has to have a purpose other than taking. If a person or object is a liability than it must be removed immediately because it will continue to cost you time and money. I asked him how can a thing be a liability? He said think of it like a vehicle you bought for your business to travel in and make deliveries. You just paid $2500.00 for it, drove it off the lot and a day later you had a flat tire and spent $500 for towing and new tire. On your way to go to make a delivery the van overheats and you have to get a new radiator. I costs you $1500.00 in parts and labor. The customer is mad because you're late with their order and to make them happy you give them a 20-percent discount on the order. This van keeps costing you money and wasted time. DeVon says this is how people and things can be liabilities in your life.

He went on to describe how to look at an asset. An asset will bring you value. Take that same van for example. Let's say you spent $5000.00 instead of $2500.00. Double the cash, so it took you months to save up, but it's a better van. Bigger motor, great suspension and even has a warranty. You pull off the lot spending more money but knowing it will make you more money. You look at an asset as an investment that will raise your value or productivity and save you time and money.

After that conversation I started to look at things differently. At the time my business was growing and I found myself stressed out with problem employees. I had created a monster in my company. I had hired a lot of employees that were friends and family members. People would come up to me and ask for a job. I felt obligated to help most times after hearing a sad story even though they didn't even have the experience to do the work. I immediately started losing money from wasted stock and even theft. I could remember feeling stuck. I wanted to help these people but they were killing my business. They were becoming major liabilities. Days had passed since DeVon and I had this conversation but I started making changes. I made two lists - one was liabilities and the other was assets - and I put each employees name and would think about if this individual was a giver or taker. The question was so simple that it made it apparent about who had to go. I was no longer stuck with guilt and I was astonished with this way of thinking.

This simple process helped me understand how I had the power to adjust any situation in my life. It has been a consistent tool that I use in every part of my life. Before I make any decisions about people that want to work with me I always ask myself if this person is going to be an asset or liability? Before I decide to undertake a new business deal with a company I ask myself is this deal going to be an asset to my growth or a liability? Being able to see things from this perspective has helped me stay on my road to success.

Only invest in assets because they will always gain value. I'm always purchasing new equipment for my companies and I use this way of thinking. Most people look at how much a product or piece of equipment costs. I look at how much money I can make off the investment. Now it makes me think twice when I see someone who is living beyond their means buying homes and cars that they can't afford to sustain. Most people would look at them as someone that is successful. Being able to tell the difference between these two principles has helped me to not get caught up on the bling and focus on objectives that will help me produce long term success and not short term distractions. True success is having the freedom to be financially free.

Ten Steps I Use to Fulfill My Goals and Objectives

1. Be clear, know what you want
2. Pre-Plan your goals and expect them to happen
3. Write down your goals
4. Take action
5. Be prepared and grind
6. Have valor and vision
7. Study
8. Keep distractions away
9. Growth
10. Succeed

Be clear, know what you want

Success is created by the thoughts you most think about. When thinking about your goals ask yourself the question "What do I want?" The universe works in non-congruent ways. If you're not precise on what you expect you never know what your success looks like. I can pass you by and you wouldn't even know it.

Pre-plan your goals and expect them to happen

Pre-planning is not only writing your goals out, it's visualizing the end result. You have to expect that your goal will be accomplished. It's not enough to plan it, you must believe in it. Create ways that help you believe deeper in your capabilities. One of the ways that you do this is to stay away from negative people. Stay around productive, positive people. When doubt approaches these people will be your support system helping you reinforce your values.

Write or draw out your goals

Write down your goals with as much detail as possible. Let your mind dream big. I'm an artist so I also draw out my goals. This creative process is amazing. It helps you fully visualize what you want.

Take action

This is sometimes the hardest part. You must make a commitment to yourself to keep moving. Stop over thinking. It will never be the right time. "You don't have to see the whole staircase. Just take the first step" - Dr. Martin Luther King, Jr.

Be prepared and grind

Always be prepared. Preparation is the key to making profits. Hard work beats talent especially if talent doesn't apply hard work. Take no short cuts. Outwork the competition. Do what others won't do and make no excuses. Work hard. Keep grinding, pushing yourself towards your success.

Have vision and valor

Vision to look past your current situations. Valor to step out in honorable faith and bring the vision to life.

Study

Listen and watch self improvement materials that will help you stay focused and motivated. Study high achievers that have had similar obstacles in life. Study how they have endured the hard times and how they became successful. Successful people leave clues to their success just got to know what to look for. Try to find a coach or mentor ASAP.

Keep distractions away

Distraction is the process of diverting the attention of an individual or group from the desired area of focus. Distractions come from both external and internal sources. External distractions include factors such as visual triggers, social interactions, music, text messages, and phone calls. There are also internal distractions such as hunger, fatigue, illness, anxiety, and daydreaming. Both external and internal distractions contribute to the loss of focus.

Growth

Growth is the only way to measure your success. You must always spend time analyzing your journey. Stop and ask yourself frequently "Am I growing." I make it a habit to ask myself weekly, monthly and yearly.

Succeed

Success can be overwhelming at times. Most people look at what society tells us what success is. Find out what success means to you. Visualize your successful lifestyle.

Ten Biggest Causes of Failure

1. Lack of definite purpose, goal, or vision
2. Lack of ambition to move past mediocrity
3. A negative mental attitude
4. Lack of self-discipline
5. Lack of a creative imagination
6. The use of race, sex, or circumstances as an excuse
7. Lack of faith in one's dream
8. Ill health
9. Lack of persistence in carrying through to finish that which you start
10. The desire to cheat the process and get something for nothing

Chapter 8

THE ART OF
SUCCESS #AOSBOOK

www.MalcolmMccrae.com

Consistency

[kənˈsistənsē]

Success is a blueprint,
failure is a habit.
Stay committed.

Ohene aniwa

One of the most important lessons I've learned was from a great friend and mentor Tony Felder, A.K.A. Tone. Tone is a six foot tall, 250 pound, big broad shouldered walking hustle machine. Tone was an entrepreneur and building contractor from Philadelphia. We hit it off one day as he entered my shop. It was about one hour before we closed and it was getting dark outside. My shop Sho' Time Wild Image was located on 38th and North Ave.; one of the roughest crime inflicted areas in Milwaukee. Tone walks in and at this specific time of the year all of the local businesses in the area are getting robbed at gunpoint.

The robbers knew the area and scoped out most of the businesses before they would rob them. Most of the crimes happened late in the evening. My neighbor down the street had just gotten robbed the night before. It was a rough time and we were prepared to possibly be the next victims. That evening we had a shop packed with customers. Tone chatted with some of the customers and staff and even began to walk some of our clients to their cars. After we closed I chatted with him and asked him why did he stay and help? He said that's what he does. I was confused. I never had anyone offer to help because that's who they are.

I was amazed that this stranger from the East Coast would put himself in danger to help my customers and community. I started to ask more questions about his business, family and this code of commitment that he had with people. Not only was he being security but he would talk with the clients making them smile and laugh. He helps people in the community. He knew about the robberies and decided to help secure our business. From that day on anytime he would drive past the shop he would stop to check on things.

I realized that he had a gift for communicating with the world. It didn't matter if you were a homeless drug addict or a single mother; he could help people lower their guard and trust him. I was so honored to have him around because no robber wanted to deal with the consequences of Tone getting a hold of them. Tone made it really clear to any person that wanted drama to think twice. I was honored what he did for the community.

Weeks later my business had a fire. The fire burned the roof and second floor of my building. I was devastated. I remember getting a call from the firefighters at 2 a.m. telling me that my business was on fire. Before they

Restoration and remodeling underway after fire devastation at Sho' Time Wild Image.

could finish their sentence, I put some clothes on and hopped in my truck to go see the damage. As I get there I see the street blocked off by police and fire trucks. They let me through the barricade where I see red hot flames coming through the roof. My two sisters, Nandi and Omotiyo and my father lived upstairs from the shop. I was so happy to see them outside and safe. It was an electrical fire and weeks earlier I had just remodeled the upstairs. I remember just standing outside and watching my dream go up in flames. The next day a million things were going on in my head.

I wasn't going to give up though. I was determined to open my company back up. I was committed to being successful and wasn't going to let anyone or anything stop me. I started to create a plan in my head. I called my friend Tone up and we began to work on repairing the damaged areas. I found a roofer would could replace the roof damage. We worked and worked and while we were repairing the building I managed to keep the orders flowing. I would work long nights drywalling and painting the walls. It was an overwhelmingly fulfilling experience. I took all of the frustration from the fire out on making my place better than ever. I finally fully opened up the doors two months later with a new look.

The key to success is consistency. Being consistent is based around everyday habits. One of those habits is what I call staying on track. As I continue to create great opportunities in my life and for my business I have to make sure that I stay on track. It's so easy to allow the mind to run free.

There have been parts of my life where I've spent large amounts of time alone building and shaping my knowledge or skill. This time could be as long as two years and as short as two days. It's a cycle of high focus and productivity. I call this getting in the zone. When I'm in the zone no one or nothing can stop or slow me down. Most times I'm working on a group of problems that I need to work out in order to grow. The zone is a magical mode and when I get in it I have to be ready to work.

As I write this book I'm in the zone. I've been writing books and painting a 12 piece collection on 5 ft. x 5 ft. canvas! I'm running my live

training events and touring. I'm also working on a large mural project that is over 1,100 sq.-ft. Last week I was in Fort Worth, Texas where I just inspired over 1,000 middle and high school students! I have a pace that I live my life. It's a high energy rhythm that I have learned works well for me. I'm always working on multiple projects in order to make things better. I get bored easily so I need to be stimulated with all parts of my creative being. For many people it may be difficult to stay energetic day after day but for me I have adapted my life so I feed off of this energy. To some it may be chaotic but for me it's the constant flow of energy that I need to feel alive.

Number Two out of Malcolm's new collection.

I push myself to be my best. I understand to be the best I have to be resilient. Being resilient is the ability to withstand or recover quickly from difficult conditions. You must be consistent at being resilient. I've overcome being homeless and hungry in my life. So when I go through hardships I know what it takes to get through an obstacle. From losing my mother as a teen to watching good friends get incarcerated or killed. I know that the only thing that I have to do is be consistent about wanting more and expecting more for myself and family. Consistency is one of those vague attributes that everyone wants, but few people actually manage to gain. I would like to share with you some steps and tools that have been a consistent positive impact in my life.

Steps and Tools that Have Been a Consistent Positive Impact in My Life

Be Realistic

Consistency is a fantastic trait and one that you should definitely work to cultivate. Remember, however, that it's a trait that can take time to practice. You won't be perfectly consistent right away. That's okay! Be kind to yourself when you screw up.

Don't make a generalized "be more consistent" plan. Trying to be more consistent in general is just going to be overwhelming. Think about what specific areas in your life require more consistency. Do you need to be consistent about your exercise habits? Do you need to be consistent about your work requirements? Your romantic relationships?

You're not going to be consistent 100% of the time. You need to be okay with making mistakes and occasionally getting lax about your consistent habits.

Build Your Willpower

You can't have consistency without improving your willpower. Consistency requires willpower to achieve, because consistency tends to lean towards going to the gym every day, even when you don't feel like it, for example. To do that, you need to have the willpower to do it.

Have tricks to boost your willpower. It's really hard to just force yourself through things and not always the best way to accomplish something. For example, if you're trying to be consistent about eating in a healthy way, make sure that you have healthy options on hand for when you're hungry, rather than just going for the unhealthy option.

Avoid situations where you will be forced to exert considerable amounts of willpower in order to be consistent. To use the healthy eating example again, don't go grocery shopping after a long, difficult day at work. You'll be more likely to just go for the fastest, easiest option (rarely the healthiest) instead of being consistent about your diet.

Make sure your actions match your words. Being consistent means that you don't say one thing while actually doing something else. You can't be inconsistent in your behavior and expect to behave consistently in other parts of your life.

For example, if you're looking to be more consistent in your friendship with others, and you tell them that you're going to be better about calling and checking in, being consistent means that you actually follow through by doing what you have said.

"Being consistent means that you don't say one thing while actually doing something else."
- Malcolm McCrae

Avoid making claims that you can't back up with your actions. There is no shame in admitting you don't yet know how to do something. For example, if you're tasked with something at work or school that you haven't done before or don't know how to do, don't pretend like you've got everything under control. Instead, ask for some assistance and show your willingness to fill in the gaps in your knowledge.

Eliminate Negative Thinking

Negative thinking is the bane of consistency and of willpower. When you think negatively you are making yourself less likely to be able to hold to your consistent actions.

Pay attention to negative thought patterns that will hinder you in the future. There are specific thoughts that have a tendency to run your life: "I can't do this," "I'm stupid, lazy, (etc., etc)."

When you do notice these negative thought patterns, turn them around or introduce a more positive or neutral thought. So, for example, if you find yourself thinking "I can't do this" instead turn it around and think "I'm going to practice doing this, even if I'm not great at it to start with."

Figure out what areas you need to work on to make yourself more likely to be consistent. Everyone has areas of themselves that could use a little work. Perhaps you're really great at being consistent at work, but at home you're constantly forgetting to do all the things you need to.

Set specific goals. General consistency is great, but being consistent is a lot easier and more likely to succeed if you set specific goals. These goals will help you behave consistently and give you something to strive for. You can set a variety of goals in different areas of your life.

Consider how you want to use consistency to achieve your specific goals. For example, if your specific goal is to lose weight, you would need to work on being consistent with exercise, with your diet (eating healthy foods), etc.

As another example: if you want to get a book published, you would need to be consistent about writing each day, about devoting time to editing, about figuring out the publishing world, and sending your manuscript off.

Hold Yourself Accountable

To be consistent you have to make sure that you recognize when you don't come up to the standards and goals that you've set. Be patient with the process. Change is a slow process. If you try to do everything at once all you're going to do is overwhelm yourself.

Tell people you trust about your goals and your attempts to be consistent about various aspects of your life. When they see you're not behaving consistently, this gives them permission to call you out.

Don't beat yourself up when you don't hit the mark. No one is perfect and no one is perfectly consistent. You aren't going to be, either. What matters is that you keep working towards your goals and towards consistency.

Plan For Failure

Everyone fails. It doesn't matter how dedicated you are, how intelligent you are, how prepared you are, you aren't always going to succeed. You have to be willing to entertain that possibility and figure out what to do if you don't succeed. How are you going to handle failure?

A lot of times the reason people fail to maintain their willpower and their consistency is because they haven't planned for failure. Individual failures mean little to your overall success (for example, getting rejected by the literary agent has only a marginal impact on your overall ability to be published).

Plan for your setbacks and failures. If that literary agent rejects your manuscript figure out where next to send it, or look it over to see what might be improved.

Remember, consistency doesn't equal perfection. For example, yes, a good writer should try to write every day. Life sometimes gets in the way, sometimes you're sick, sometimes you simply don't write. If you start beating yourself up for not writing, you'll make yourself less rather than more likely to be consistent.

Use Critical Visualization

Visualization can actually aid you a lot if you use it properly. You want to use realistic visualization. Visualize yourself accomplishing your goal. Think about how it will feel, the pleasure and satisfaction to see your dream come true. Don't consider the obstacles and setbacks that you may face.

Daydreaming can also be useful, as long as you limit your time doing it. Give your mind time to range freely each night before you go to bed. This can help you process and assess situations, and help you to keep your consistency and goals, because you'll come up with ways to get past the potential obstacles that might keep you from gaining this skill.

As a speaker I keep myself from getting nervous by visualizing a standing ovation. I focus in on how I will feel after the speech. I tell myself it's only 45 minutes which helps me to stay focused and reflect on how the time will go by fast. Every time I use my visualization tool before I know it I'm out there on stage having fun.

Increase Your Motivation

If you don't stay motivated, you won't make those changes in your life that allow you to be consistent. You'll fall back into old, destructive patterns of behavior, instead of sticking with the new patterns you're trying to create.

Don't tell yourself "I'm not motivated" or even "I'm not feeling motivated today." The more you skip days when you're trying to instill new patterns of thought in yourself, the less likely you are to succeed. Instead, tell yourself "I'm going to practice being motivated today even if I don't feel like it." If you're having a difficult day and you don't want to, for example, do any writing, do less than you normally do. If you write for an hour, cut that down to half an hour, or only write a paragraph instead of a page.

Don't try to do too many things at one time. Sort your different goals out one or two at a time. If you're trying to finish your manuscript and improve your consistency at work and get into shape, you're going to burn out quickly. Instead, work on improving your work ethic and your writing ethic, before adding your exercise ethic.

Remind yourself why consistency is important to you. What is it you're trying to accomplish by being consistent? What happens if you fail to be consistent? Keeping these things in mind when you're trying to accomplish your goals and be consistent.

Own Your Path

Your consistency is built around your goals. There will be people that will come into your life that will try to choose your path for you. These goals are tools created to help you remember your dream and to stay on track. Everyone's path is different and unique to them. It is up to each of us to find our own path. Only you can live your life and receive the success that comes with it.

Stay true to what you believe and never feel ashamed of your dreams, ambitions or goals.

Don't allow your focus to be distracted by cheating or using short cuts. There are no shortcuts to success. Each path is meant to prepare you for your true success.

Beware of any get rich fast schemes. Totally run the opposite way from any person that is associated to that way of thinking. Every year hundreds of thousands of people lose tons of time and money trying to find ways to cheat their way to success. There is no such thing as fast, easy success.

Dream

Have a desire or idea that is bigger than yourself. Every successful person starts with a dream. Dream and dream big. It is not your business to know the path or how you will accomplish this idea, it is your responsibility to maintain your dream and believe in it until it comes to flourish.

For example, when my dad and brother and I were homeless we dreamed about having a successful family business. We didn't know how but that didn't stop us from dreaming. Six years later we created a six figure business empire. Use your dream as an opportunity to push yourself.

Wash, Rinse, Repeat

This analogy used to indicate the continual repetition of an action or sequence of events, typically in a way regarded as tiresomely predictable.

"Find a system that works. Make the system work for you. Don't work for the system. Repeat the system over and over, with an expectation of knowing the results." - Malcolm McCrae

These principles have helped me stay consistent in my life. It can be hard at times but it's a habit that we all have to work on. The more I'm committed to a project the more I take pride in seeing it's success. It is a natural law of the universe, the Law of Attraction. The more one thinks about a particular situation the more the situation starts to manifest in one's life. It is a science that deals with a cycle of life.

Nature is a great example of this. I use nature as a tool in my life to help me make sense of situations. Nature is a consistent cycle - like farmers who grow crops off the land by planting seeds, nurturing them and watching them grow. This pattern or cycle is how we have to look at our lives. We have to be consistent when cultivating our dreams just like the farmer is consistent when cultivating the soil to grow his crop.

I've learned three principles of consistency from watching mother nature. Use these to help become more consistent in your life...

Plant It

Plant your dream or idea deep with inside yourself. Appreciate it's value and trust it will grow.

Nurture It

Protect your idea and dream. Give it time everyday to blossom and be prepared to make it happen. Learn the skills necessary to give it what is needed to grow. Take action now. Don't over think it. Do it.

Watch It Grow

This is the time when your expectations and work have come together to start seeing results. This part is built around being patient, staying committed and having courage. Most people give up right before the breakthrough is about to happen.

Chapter 9

THE ART OF **SUCCESS** #AOSBOOK

www.MalcolmMccrae.com

Entrepreneurship
[en·tre·pre·neur·ship]

The activity of setting up
a business or businesses.
Taking on financial risks to make a profit.

Okuafo Pa

In my career I have created businesses products and services that have grossed over $500,000. I'm so fortunate to have lived a lifestyle of an entrepreneur. I started on the street corner homeless in Columbus, Ohio, moving to a position where I have authored five books and produced over 10 DVDs and instructional courses. One of my passions has been speaking across the world to students, educators and at corporate functions.

I describe entrepreneurship as a lifestyle. It's a life changing choice he or she makes. It's freedom to live a self sufficient lifestyle. A lifestyle entrepreneur focuses more on the life rewards provided to people that enjoy and have a passion for what they are doing. An individual that creates a business with the purpose of altering their personal lifestyle and not for the sole purpose of making profits. An entrepreneur is a problem solver that is compensated by sharing how he or she solved the problem. Entrepreneurs and small businesses produce services or products that are sold to customers and consumers.

According to the SBA (Small Business Administration)...

There are 28 million small businesses in America
and they account for 54% of all U.S. sales.

Small businesses provide 55% of all jobs
and 66% of all net new jobs since the 1970s.

The 600,000 plus franchised small businesses in the U.S. account for 40% of all retail sales and provide jobs for some 8 million people.

The small business sector in America occupies 30-50% of all commercial space, an estimated 20-34 billion square feet.

Entrepreneurship and the small business sector is growing rapidly, while corporate America has been "downsizing", the rate of small business "start-ups" has grown, and the rate for small business failures has declined.

The number of small businesses in the United States
has increased 49% since 1982.

Since 1990, as big business eliminated 4 million jobs,
small businesses and entrepreneurship added 8 million new jobs.

Four Traits of an Entrepreneur

Entrepreneurship is a Way of Thinking. Start Young

The world needs new entrepreneurs. Entrepreneurs create jobs, lift the standard of living, usher new technology into society, and keep competition alive in the marketplace.

Entrepreneurs have created a culture or lifestyle especially with the boom of entrepreneurs from the ages of 20-35. With the Internet becoming more accessible and faster it has given like minded creatives, visionaries and dreamers the ability to have the freedom that entrepreneurship brings. Starting a business is difficult, and it's crucial that the next generation has as much knowledge as possible.

As the CEO of a successful startup myself, I have decades of experience launching both brick and mortar businesses and online companies. I've been through the ups and downs of business. I know what it takes to make it. If I could go back and give my twenty something self a bit of advice about starting out as an entrepreneur, these are the tips I'd start with.

Entrepreneur is a Problem Solver

An entrepreneur looks at a problem and knows it's an opportunity to get paid if you can be the one to solve it. Successful entrepreneurs focus their energy on providing creative solutions to the problem solving process. The bigger the problem the more people will pay for the solution. Every good product solves some sort of problem. This solution can be a product or service that one charges a fee for. If you want to be a successful entrepreneur, your natural response to any given problem should always be to ask yourself how can you solve that problem. Problem-solving becomes a habit. As you become alert to problems with no solutions, you become alert to new ways to create, grow, develop, and innovate new products or services.

An Entrepreneur Takes Calculated Risks

Risk sensitive people don't make very good entrepreneurs. We have a saying "Scared money don't make money." Neither do extremely reckless people who leap first and look later. Real entrepreneurs evaluate their potential risks. They also know how to minimize the risks they need to take through hard work, dedication, and strategic planning. When a risk goes bad an entrepreneur doesn't waste a lot of time looking for someone to blame. Instead a true entrepreneur analyzes what went wrong, learns from it, and moves on.

An Entrepreneur is Self-Motivated

This is about more than simply being your own boss. This is about more than simply being able to get up in the morning and get to work. An entrepreneur is always capable of seeing potential in most situations. The daily objective is not about being satisfied, sure you want to be able enjoy the fruits of your labor but that's not the main focus. The business mindset keeps one looking forward to creating more opportunities. It's an inner push

Malcolm's portable airbrush shop shown here at liquidation sales. Not only was he an accomplished artist in his own right but realized he must supplement his income by taking his wares to other markets across the country.

to find the next points of success. An entrepreneur is also willing to push their self always looking at what more they can do to achieve the main objectives or goals. Last year's success was fine, but this year's success should reflect growth always looking for ways to make the vision successful. As Janet Jackson famously stated, "What have you done for me lately."

Entrepreneurship

As a boy I always had characteristics of an entrepreneur. My mother and father raised us to look at money as a tool. I was always around business men and women growing up. These entrepreneurs owned all kinds of businesses; from barbershops to day care centers, even bookstores. I was always obsessed with having my own.

Being the oldest of five kids I knew that I would have to buy my own things. I started my own business as soon as I was old enough to count money. I would study how people spent money and how these business owners took pride in their products or services. I learned how to talk and socialize with people and how to get my point across without being "salesy". My favorite customers were women because I knew if they could see my smile then I would have them hooked. As soon as a customer would look interested I would show the biggest smile on my face and the women would say he is so cute and "he has dimples." When I heard that comment I knew I was going to get a sale.

The first sale is the hardest. It's the icebreaker. It sets the pace of the day. One of my first business endeavors was selling incense door to door. Incense sold for one dollar for a bag of 20 sticks. My father and I formed this business.

One day I came and asked for an allowance and my dad made it real clear to me that money had to be earned. Money is a principle that is built around two people agreeing on a transaction. At first this idea was foreign to me so my dad explained it in a way I would understand. He said that money is a tool and to use it as that. He explained to me that I could earn the money I wanted by creating a business. "A business?" I thought to myself. I'm only a kid. How do I start a business? I began to ask how and he handed me a bag of incense. I totally didn't understand. That day my dad and I became business partners. My father then explained the concepts of business to me.

The first thing he said is that you must have a product or service that people will pay you for. Your product or service must have value that the customers can easily see. Success in business is built around a great product and great salesmanship. As a salesperson you have to get good at letting the potential client know why he or she should buy this product.

My father had a t-shirt screen printing business. He would design t-shirts and sell them at numerous local and regional events. I would watch how he would use different sale techniques to close the sale. My father had a pitch for any customer. He always let his natural charisma shine through. He would say that you must take the time to have an attractive display. How you displayed your products shows the customer that you appreciate and respect yourself and your business. Your display and presentation can make or break a sale. If people see that you care about your service or product then they will care.

Another important tool that my father explained to me is attitude. You have to have a good attitude to make good money. If a customer sees a depressed, sad person or a person that doesn't believe or have confidence in themselves most will be reluctant to buy. If they like you they will spend and if you can make them laugh then you will get the cash. My dad would always say that everyone can sell. You sell yourself to the world everyday. When you recommend a movie to someone you are selling that movie. The key is all about sharing the experience. This is why in business most will say that word of mouth is the best marketing tool.

Here are some business terms that I learned early in my entrepreneurial journey...

Customer

One that purchases a commodity or service.

Wholesaler

Goods sold in large quantities at low prices to be retailed by others. My father knew a guy in Chicago who would wholesale incense in bulk to us a bundles of incense cost $10 for 1,000 sticks.

Markup

The amount added to the cost price of goods to cover overhead and profit. We would take a 1,000 stick bundle and break it down to 50 bundles with 20 sticks in each pack. We sold the individual bags for $1.

Profit

The profit is what is left over after your initial investment was recouped. It's the financial gain, the difference between the amount earned and the amount spent.

Here is the simple math:
Cost for 1,000 sticks of incense $10. Fifty sticks make a resale pack for $1. We make 50 packs from the bundle which equals $50.
The initial investment was $10 so the profit is $40.

Reinvest

After all of the incense is sold you must invest in more stock in order to keep turning over income and profits.

This procedure is repeated over and over again to maintain consistent business. When my father explained this concept to me a light bulb went off. It was as simple as washing clothes. Wash, rinse repeat was the key to success with repeat results. At that moment I realized that I enjoyed business and the money it generated. The simple philosophy of how business is run was incredible to me and I never wanted to work for anyone ever again. I became a master at sales. It became easier to me the more I did it. I would practice my pitch in the mirror just to make sure I was ready for any excuse a customer would use.

Being around so many entrepreneurs also gave me the confidence needed. I knew it was all about the odds. I knew if I could get a "yes" that would be all I needed to get the ball rolling. I started to see a flow after I would break the ice with getting my first sale. Then I could use that confidence as momentum to get another and another. I was all about the effort and attitude. I had a great smile and charisma so I became really successful.

Being a successful business person takes courage because most people get discouraged after they hear the first "no," but at this young age I learned that you have to ignore the "no's" and focus in on the yeses. That's all that counts.

Let me tell you about an entrepreneur that focused on "yes" and didn't take "no" for an answer. She became the first women in the history of America to be a self made millionaire. Her name was Sarah Breedlove (December 23, 1867 – May 25, 1919). Known as Madam C. J. Walker, she was an African-American entrepreneur, philanthropist, as well as a political and social activist. Eulogized as the first female self-made millionaire in America, she became one of the wealthiest African-American women in the country, the world's most successful female entrepreneur of her time, and one of the most successful African-American business owners ever.

Madame C.J. Walker, the first female self-made millionaire in America, became one of the wealthiest African-American women in the country, the world's most successful female entrepreneur of her time, and one of the most successful African-American business owners ever.

Walker made her fortune by developing and marketing a line of beauty and hair products for black women through the Madame C.J. Walker Manufacturing Company, the successful business she founded. Walker was also known for her philanthropy and activism. She made financial donations to numerous organizations and became a patron of the arts. Villa Lewaro, Walker's lavish estate in Irvington-on-Hudson, New York, served as a social gathering place for the African-American community.

Her path wasn't easy. During the 1880s, Madam C. J. Walker lived in a community where ragtime music was developed—she sang at the St. Paul African Methodist Episcopal Church and started to yearn for an educated life as she watched the community of women at her church. Ms. Walker found work as a laundress, barely earning more than a dollar a day, but she was determined to make enough money to provide her daughter with a formal education. As was common among black women of her era, Sarah experienced severe dandruff and other scalp ailments, including baldness, due to skin disorders and the application of harsh products such as lye that were included in soaps to cleanse hair and wash clothes. Other contributing factors to her hair loss included poor diet, illnesses, and infrequent bathing and hair washing during a time when most Americans lacked indoor plumbing, central heating and electricity. She began to experiment with both home remedies and store-bought hair care treatments in an attempt to improve her condition. She finally came up with a formula that started to heal the scalp and made her hair grow longer and healthier.

Most people say that she was in the hair growing business but Madam C. J. Walker believed she was is in the healthy scalp business. In 1907, Walker and her husband traveled around the South and Southeast promoting her products and giving lecture demonstrations of her "Walker Method"—involving her own formula for pomade, brushing and the use of heated combs.

Between 1911 and 1919, during the height of her career, Walker and her company employed several thousand women as sales agents for its products. By 1917 the company had trained nearly 20,000 women. Dressed in a characteristic uniform of white shirts and black skirts and carrying black satchels, they visited houses around the United States and in the Caribbean offering Walker's hair pomade and other products packaged in tin containers carrying her image. Walker understood the power of advertising and brand awareness. Heavy advertising, primarily in African-American newspapers and magazines, in addition to Walker's frequent travels to promote her products, helped make Walker and her products well known in the United States. Walker became even more widely known by the 1920s as her business market expanded beyond the United States to Cuba, Jamaica, Haiti, Panama, and Costa Rica.

In addition to training in sales and grooming, Walker showed other black women how to budget and build their own businesses, as well as encouraging them to become financially independent. In 1917, inspired by the model of the National Association of Colored Women, Walker began organizing her sales agents into state and local clubs. The result was the establishment of the National Beauty Culturists and Benevolent Association of Madam C. J. Walker Agents (predecessor to the Madam C. J. Walker Beauty Culturists Union of America). Its first annual conference convened in Philadelphia during the summer of 1917 with 200 attendees. The conference is believed to have been among the first national gatherings of women entrepreneurs to discuss business and commerce. During the convention Walker gave prizes to women who had sold the most products and brought in the most new sales agents. She also rewarded those who made the largest contributions to charities in their communities.

Make it Yourself

Don't be scared to make it. An entrepreneur's mindset is built around getting things done. Most times someone has done what you want to accomplish. Sometimes you will find yourself having to create a process or product from scratch. This is the case when you feel limited or the ingredients are too expensive or hard to get. I have always been a fan of making my own products from scratch. To this day I still purchase equipment and learn skills that help me produce my own products.

For years I would have other people produce my DVDs and videos and every project I would spend a lot of money and time on people who wouldn't take my projects serious. So I started to invest in equipment that would allow me to produce my own DVDs and videos in house. I then ordered videos that taught me how to use video editing software. I invested in my mind and materials that will help me grow. I learned how to film my own videos, edit them and even duplicate and package them. I use this method on everything that I do. I will invest in the know how just so I understand the process. Sometimes it's cheaper for me to outsource and sometimes it makes sense to create it in house. The key is that I have options to change and update things ASAP. I like to be able to understand how things work especially in my business. I find some of my most inspiring breakthroughs by just doing it and learning from trial and error. Life has showed me that people will tell you what you can't do but you will never know until you try it for yourself.

Malcolm was awarded this Certificate of Achievement and Award of Excellence for Best Marketing Program by the Milwaukee School of Entrepreneurship at the Second Annual Young Entrepreneur Conference and Business Competition March 23-24, 1999 in Milwaukee, WI.

I have been an entrepreneur all of my life and there is no other feeling in the world than to be a self made success. Is it easy? Of course not. This decision is a lifestyle that is full of incredible highs and scary lows but it is the freedom that keeps me loving this journey. I have made a lot of money and lost a lot as well. But I realized that I don't do what I do for money. Everyday I wake up in the morning inspired to be the best that I can be and to build companies and brands that help inspire others to be the best version of themselves. That is my quest and journey in life and entrepreneurship has helped me do that. I hope you choose to use it in your life to accomplish your dreams of success.

Chapter 10

THE ART
SUCCESS #AOSBOOK

www.MalcolmMccrae.com

Leadership
[lee-der-ship]

The position or function of a leader.
A person who guides or directs a group.

Nea ope se obedi hene

"My principles are more important than the money or my title."
-Muhammad Ali

"ALI" WWW.MALCOLMMCCRAE.COM 2016

135

Qualities That Make Great Leaders

Integrity

Inspiration

Innovation

Authenticity

Confidence

Concentration

Communication

Empowerment

Patience

Positivity

Integrity
The quality of being honest and having strong moral principles
Integrity is the development of having good character
Try to do the right thing because it is right

Inspiration
The process of being mentally stimulated to do something creative

Innovation
The action or process of a new method, idea, product, etc

Authenticity
Representing one's true nature or beliefs

Confidence
Belief in oneself and one's powers or abilities

Concentration
The action or power of focusing one's attention or mental effort

Communication
The imparting or exchanging of information

Empowerment
The process of becoming stronger and more confident,
especially in controlling one's life and claiming one's rights

Patience
The state of endurance under difficult circumstances
Delayed gratification

Positivity
The practice of being or tendency to be positive or optimistic in attitude

How to Bring Out the True Leader Inside of You

Some of us are born leaders while others have to learn leadership traits or skills. I was a born leader, always outgoing, adventurous, creative, smart, and opinionated. Then I started going to school and everything changed. I wasn't supposed to be any of those things -- I was supposed to be quiet and well behaved. I could remember being in class with all the other students who were mostly well to do white kids. I was always one of a hand full of blacks in my class and I can remember the feeling of being stuck in a box where I couldn't let my personality shine. I was a creative leader and that wasn't acceptable, especially to my teacher and principal. They made it clear time after time. I know that it was because I was an African American male student who was outgoing and smart and I would help the other kids who had learning challenges.

Malcolm and his mother, Jerryn Barnwell, pregnant with twin brother and sister.

I went to school at Hartford Avenue elementary which was one of the highest ranked schools in Milwaukee. It was hard to get in, there was always a waiting list of parents that wanted to enroll their children. It was a public school that was ran like a private school. My mom's cousin worked there as a teacher so I was able to get enrolled without a problem. Around that time, I was taught by teachers that said what I was doing was wrong. "I shouldn't be so outgoing or opinionated," the teacher said. I should give the other kids a chance to answer questions.

My mom worked at the university across the street as a cook. It was very convenient for her to pick me up after school. I remember when I was about eight, I was finally able to take the school bus home. The bus leader took me aside and told me that no one wanted to hear my opinions, and that I should just keep them to myself. Around that time, my peers let me know that "leadership" was a thing to be ridiculed and not respected. They would make remarks like "What do you think, you're better than us?" I was physically attacked, pushed down and choked for the first time in second grade. My peers thought it was fun, and funny, to steal my things and ruin them. Break my pencils, rip pages out of my sketchbooks. I was a really small kid. I didn't know how to protect myself. I was also a strong minded kid and I was the oldest out of five brothers and sisters. I had to be a leader for my little brother and sisters. They gave me the strength and courage that I needed to deal with the bullying. I knew that I had to take the harsh ridicule in order to protect them from that pain and humiliation that I was enduring. I now realize that one of the most important traits as a leader is to know how to help and protect the helpless and the people you love and care about.

Leadership = Pops and Clayborn

As I was writing this book I had to add this chapter about the leadership that is required in fatherhood. This became really apparent when I was doing a workshop for a school in my hometown. I was invited by a man named Clayborn Benson to conduct a talk for third graders at Brown Street Academy. Mr. Benson directed and founded the Black Historical Society in Milwaukee. It was a building that has always held community events from Kwanzaa to marriages. My family and I have been going to these community events at the Historical Society for over 20 years, so I knew Mr. Benson very well. He asked me to come talk to these young people at a school where he works at once a week. I came in

Malcolm and Pops in Ft. Worth, TX where Malcolm recently spoke to 1,400 students at Paul Laurence Dunbar High School and Wedgwood Middle School students over two days as he presented the Art of Success workshop.

and did my presentation and the kids loved it. Afterwards, we started to break down the equipment, and helped Mr. Clayborn load the PA system into his car, he stopped me and said, "I admire your father, he helped me become a better father for my daughter." I paused and asked him to explain what he meant. He said, "I've watched you and all four of your siblings grow up. When your mom died I watched your dad step up to the plate and raise all of you. I know it wasn't easy for him, especially with your sister."

He was referring to my sister Omotiyo. She had cerebral palsy and we would always be the family with the wheelchair strapped to a cab or the car trunk. He went on to say that not one time did he ever see my dad complain or ever give up on raising his five kids. I asked Mr. Benson, "You remember that?" "Yes", he said. It was at a time when he was having issues with his relationship with his daughter. Watching my dad with five kids, including Omotiyo who was disabled, gave him strength to realize that if my dad could do it then he could do it, too. My father is a no excuse type of person. He doesn't believe in the word impossible. He's always raised his kids to be leaders and have a sense of respect for yourself and other people, especially family. But I never thought that his actions were being watched in the community.

Talking to Clayborn Benson I now realize that fatherhood is one of the best examples of leadership in the world. If you look at the poorest communities in America; the communities that suffer from drugs, lack of education and low income housing you will find the lack of fathers in the household. We're talking about even the lack of men or males that are brothers, grandfathers, uncles etc. We have a major gap missing in these communities and that gap creates a lack of leadership. I travel the country talking to young boys in schools all over the country and the one thing that I've noticed is that the young boys that don't have fathers around are more likely to get involved with gangs, selling drugs, dying or being incarcerated. The young men that have a father, uncle or male figure in their lives are more confident, deal with pressure better and have a sense of respect for themselves and others. It's a situation that is common from state to state, school to school. Even when I look at my own life I had my dad around most of my adolescent life. I have friends that have never seen their father or never even had a man in their family that they could look up to for leadership.

One of the things you want to do is be confident in your thoughts of leadership. When it is your time to lead, be proud and dig deep inside yourself and be loyal to your leadership abilities. Most think of loyalty as being loyal to a person. To me the most important thing is loyalty to myself. It can be looked at as an ego problem, but loyalty is a tool that can be used to help you define and produce greatness within sight. I have a creed I stay loyal to; living, creating, and inspiring. It is a mindset that I have adapted to help me stay focused on who I am and what I expect in life. I had to understand that my success was built around my honesty with loyalty to myself. There have been many situations in my personal and business life that have questioned my loyalty. I'm honored to say that I have been successful at staying true to who I am.

*"That strong mother doesn't tell
her cub, son, stay weak
so the wolves can get you.
She says, toughen up,
this is reality we are living in."*
-Lauryn Hill

(LAURYN HILL) ©WWW.MALCOLMMCCRAE.COM 2015

143

APPENDIX

The Adinkra symbols are believed to have their origin from Gyaman, a former kingdom in today's Côte D'Ivoire.[1]

The Adinkra symbols express various themes that relate to the history, beliefs and philosophy of the Asante. They mostly have rich proverbial meaning since proverbs play an important role in the Asante culture. The use of Proverbs is considered as a mark of wisdom.

The Adinkra symbols continue to change as new influences impact on Ghanaian culture as some of the symbols now record specific technological developments.

On the following page is a table displaying the Adinkra symbols used to identify chapter concepts in this book. They have been arranged by names in Twi, literal translation in English and significance.

---

[1] ADINKRA - Cultural Symbols of the Asante people, compiled by Valentina A. Tetteh, NCC, St. Lawrence University, www.stlawu.edu/gallery/education/f/09textiles/adinkra_symbols.pdf

	Symbol Name	Literal Meaning	Symbol Meaning
Chapter 1	Hye Wonnye	That which cannot be burnt	Imperishability, Endless
Chapter 2	Sesa woruban	Change your life	Transformation
Chapter 3	Nkyinkyim	Zigzag, Twisting	Adaptability, Toughness
Chapter 4	Nssa	Woven cloth, Blanket	Excellence, Authority
Chapter 5	Boa me na me boa wo	Help me to help you	Cooperation, Interdependence
Chapter 6	Tabon	Paddle	Courage
Chapter 7	Akoben	War Horn	Readiness, Preparation
Chapter 8	Ohene aniwa	King's Eye	Consistency, Vigilance
Chapter 9	Okuafu Pa	Good Farmer	Entrepreneurship
Chapter 10	Nea ope se obedi bene	He who wants to be king	Leadership

72975419R00082

Made in the USA
Columbia, SC
03 July 2017